Ruby
Pocket Reference

Michael Fitzgerald

O'REILLY®

Beijing · Cambridge · Farnham · Köln · Paris · Sebastopol · Taipei · Tokyo

Ruby Pocket Reference
by Michael Fitzgerald

Copyright © 2007 Michael Fitzgerald. All rights reserved.
Printed in Canada.

Published by O'Reilly Media, Inc., 1005 Gravenstein Highway North,
Sebastopol, CA 95472.

O'Reilly books may be purchased for educational, business, or sales
promotional use. Online editions are also available for most titles
(*safari.oreilly.com*). For more information, contact our corporate/
institutional sales department: (800) 998-9938 or *corporate@oreilly.com*.

Editor: Simon St.Laurent	**Cover Designer:** Karen Montgomery
Production Editor: Rachel Monaghan	**Interior Designer:** David Futato
Proofreader: Rachel Monaghan	**Illustrators:** Robert Romano and Jessamyn Read
Indexer: Ellen Troutman Zaig	

Printing History:

July 2007:   First Edition.

ISBN-10: 0-596-51481-6
ISBN-13: 978-0-596-51481-5
[TM]

Contents

Ruby Pocket Reference

Ruby is an open source, object-oriented programming language created by Yukihiro "Matz" Matsumoto. First released in Japan in 1995, Ruby has gained worldwide acceptance as an easy-to-learn, powerful, and expressive language, especially since the advent of Ruby on Rails, a web application framework written in Ruby (*http://www.rubyonrails.org*). Ruby's core is written in the C programming language and runs on all major platforms. It is an interpreted rather than compiled language. For more information on Ruby, see *http://www.ruby-lang.org*.

Conventions Used in This Book

The following font conventions are used in this book:

Italic

> Indicates pathnames and filenames (such as program names); Internet addresses, such as domain names and URLs; and emphasized or newly defined terms.

`Constant width`

> Indicates commands and options that should be typed verbatim in a file or in *irb*; or names and keywords in Ruby programs, including method, variable, and class names.

`Constant width italic`

> Indicates user-supplied values.

`Constant width bold`

> Used to draw attention to parts of programs.

Comments and Questions

Please address comments and questions concerning this book to the publisher:

O'Reilly Media, Inc.
1005 Gravenstein Highway North
Sebastopol, CA 95472
800-998-9938 (in the United States or Canada)
707-829-0515 (international or local)
707-829-0104 (Fax)

There is a web page for this book, which lists errata, examples, or any additional information. You can access this page at:

http://www.oreilly.com/catalog/9780596514815

To comment or ask technical questions about this book, send email to:

bookquestions@oreilly.com

For information about books, conferences, Resource Centers, and the O'Reilly Network, see the O'Reilly web site at:

http://www.oreilly.com

Acknowledgments

This book is dedicated to John H. Atkinson, Jr. (1934–2007).

I want to thank Simon St.Laurent, Ryan Waldron, and Rachel Monaghan for their help in creating, editing, and producing this book.

Running Ruby

Test to see whether Ruby is running on your computer by typing the following at a shell or command prompt:

```
ruby --version
```

An affirmative response will look similar to this (this example is for version 1.8.6 running on Mac OS X):

```
ruby 1.8.6 (2007-03-13 patchlevel 0) [powerpc-darwin8.9.0]
```

You can install Ruby on any of the major platforms. For Ruby file archives and installation instructions, see *http://www.ruby-lang.org/en/downloads*.

Running the Ruby Interpreter

Usage:

```
ruby [switches] [--] [program filename] [arguments]
```

Switches (or command-line options):

-0[*octal*]
 Specify a record separator (\0 if no argument).

-a
 Autosplit mode with -n or -p (splits $_ into $F).

-c
 Check syntax only.

-C*directory*
 cd to directory before executing your script or program.

-d
 Set debugging flags (set predefined variable $DEBUG to true).

-e '*command*'
 Execute one line of script. Several -es allowed. Omit [*program filename*].

-F*pattern*
 split( ) pattern for autosplit (-a).

-i[*extension*]
 Edit ARGV files in place (make backup if extension supplied).

-I*directory*
 Specify $LOAD_PATH (predefined variable) directory; may be used more than once.

-K*kcode*
> Specify the character set. See Table 16.

-l
> Enable line-ending processing.

-n
> Assume 'while gets(); ... end' loop around your script.

-p
> Assume loop like -n but print line also like sed.

-r*library*
> Require the library before executing your script.

-s
> Enable some switch parsing for switches after script name.

-S
> Look for the script using PATH environment variable.

-T[*level*]
> Turn on tainting checks.

-v
> Print version number, then turn on verbose mode (compare --version).

-w
> Turn warnings on for your script or program.

-W[*level*]
> Set warning level: 0=silence, 1=medium, and 2=verbose (default).

-x[*directory*]
> Strip off text before #! shebang line, and optionally cd to directory.

--copyright
> Print the copyright.

--version
> Print the version (compare -v).

Using a Shebang Line on Unix/Linux

A shebang line may appear on the first line of a Ruby program (or other program or script). Its job is to help a Unix/Linux system execute the commands in the program or script according to a specified interpreter—Ruby, in our case. (This does not work on Windows.) Here is a program named *hi.rb* with a shebang on the first line:

```
#!/usr/bin/env ruby

puts "Hello, Matz!"
```

Other alternative shebang lines are #!/usr/bin/ruby or #!/usr/local/bin/ruby. With a shebang in place, you can type the filename (followed by Return or Enter) at a shell prompt without invoking the Ruby interpreter directly:

```
$ hi.rb
```

Associating File Types on Windows

Windows doesn't know or care about shebang (#!), but you can achieve a similar effect by creating a file type association with the assoc and ftype commands on Windows (DOS). To find out whether an association exists for the file extension *.rb*, use the assoc command:

```
C:\Ruby Code>assoc .rb
File association not found for extension .rb
```

If it's not found, associate the *.rb* extension with a file type:

```
C:\Ruby Code>assoc .rb=rbFile
```

Then test to see whether the association exists:

```
C:\Ruby Code>assoc .rb
.rb=rbFile
```

Now test to see whether the file type for Ruby exists:

```
C:\Ruby Code>ftype rbfile
File type 'rbfile' not found or no open command associated
with it.
```

If not found, you can create it with a command like this:

```
C:\Ruby Code>ftype rbfile="C:\Program Files\Ruby\bin\
ruby.exe" "%1" %*
```

Be sure to put the correct path to the executable for the Ruby interpreter, followed by the substitution variables. %1 is a substitution variable for the file you want to run, and %* accepts all other parameters that may appear on the command line. Test it:

```
C:\Ruby Code>ftype rbfile
rbfile="C:\Program Files\Ruby\bin\ruby.exe" "%1" %*
```

Finally, add .rb to the PATHEXT environment variable. See whether it is there already with set:

```
C:\Ruby Code>set PATHEXT
PATHEXT=.COM;.EXE;.BAT;.CMD;.VBS;.VBE;.JS;.JSE;.WSF;.WSH;
.tcl
```

If it is not there, add it like this:

```
C:\Ruby Code>set PATHEXT=.rb;%PATHEXT%
```

Then test it again:

```
C:\Ruby Code>set PATHEXT
PATHEXT=.rb;.COM;.EXE;.BAT;.CMD;.VBS;.VBE;.JS;.JSE;.WSF;
.WSH;.tcl
```

All is now in order:

```
C:\Ruby Code>type hi.rb
#!/usr/bin/env ruby

puts "Hello, Matz!"
```

Make sure you are able to execute the file:

```
C:\Ruby Code>cacls hi.rb /g username:f
Are you sure (Y/N)?y
processed file: C:\Ruby Code\hi.rb
```

Run the program by entering the program's file name at the command prompt, with or without the file extension:

```
C:\Ruby Code>hi
Hello, Matz!
```

To preserve these settings, you may add these commands to your *autoexec.bat* file, or set the environment variables by selecting Star → Control Panel → System, clicking on the Advanced tab, and then clicking the Environment Variables button.

Reserved Words

Table 1 lists Ruby's reserved words or keywords.

Table 1. Ruby's reserved words

Reserved word	Description
BEGIN	Code, enclosed in { }, to run before the program runs.
END	Code, enclosed in { }, to run when the program ends.
alias	Creates an alias for an existing method, operator, or global variable.
and	Logical operator; same as && except and has lower precedence.
begin	Begins a code block or group of statements; closes with end.
break	Terminates a while or until loop, or a method inside a block.
case	Compares an expression with a matching when clause; closes with end. See when.
class	Defines a class; closes with end.
def	Defines a method; closes with end.
defined?	A special operator that determines whether a variable, method, super method, or block exists.
do	Begins a block, and executes code in that block; closes with end.
else	Executes following code if previous conditional is not true, set with if, elsif, unless, or case. See if, elsif.
elsif	Executes following code if previous conditional is not true, set with if or elsif.
end	Ends a code block (group of statements) started with begin, class, def, do, if, etc.

Table 1. Ruby's reserved words (continued)

Reserved word	Description
ensure	Always executes at block termination; use after last rescue.
false	Logical or Boolean false; instance of FalseClass; a pseudovariable. See true.
for	Begins a for loop; used with in.
if	Executes code block if conditional statement is true. Closes with end. Compare unless, until.
in	Used with for loop. See for.
module	Defines a module; closes with end.
next	Jumps to the point immediately before the evaluation of the loop's conditional. Compare redo.
nil	Empty, uninitialized, or invalid; always false, but not the same as zero; object of NilClass; a pseudovariable.
not	Logical operator; same as !.
or	Logical operator; same as || except or has lower precedence.
redo	Jumps after a loop's conditional. Compare next.
rescue	Evaluates an expression after an exception is raised; used before ensure.
retry	When called outside of rescue, repeats a method call; inside rescue, jumps to top of block (begin).
return	Returns a value from a method or block. May be omitted, but method or block always return a value, whether it is explicit or not.
self	Current object (receiver invoked by a method); a pseudovariable.
super	Calls method of the same name in the superclass. The *superclass* is the parent of this class.
then	Separator used with if, unless, when, case, and rescue. May be omitted, unless conditional is all on one line.
true	Logical or Boolean true; instance of TrueClass; a pseudovariable. See false.
undef	Makes a method undefined in the current class.
unless	Executes code block if conditional statement is false. Compare if, until.

Table 1. Ruby's reserved words (continued)

Reserved word	Description
until	Executes code block while conditional statement is `false`. Compare `if`, `unless`.
when	Starts a clause (one or more) under `case`.
while	Executes code while the conditional statement is true.
yield	Executes the block passed to a method.
__FILE__	Name of current source file; a pseudovariable.
__LINE__	Number of current line in the current source file; a pseudovariable.

Operators

Table 2 lists all of Ruby's operators in descending order of precedence. Operators that are implemented as methods may be overridden and are indicated in the Method column.

Table 2. Ruby's operators

Operator	Description	Method
::	Scope resolution	
[] []=	Reference, set	✓
**	Raise to power (exponentiation)	✓
+ - ! ~	Positive (unary), negative (unary), logical negation, complement	✓ (not !)
* / %	Multiplication, division, modulo (remainder)	✓
+ -	Addition, subtraction	✓
<< >>	Shift left, shift right	✓
&	Bitwise *and*	✓
| ^	Bitwise *or*, bitwise exclusive *or*	✓
> >= < <=	Greater than, greater than or equal to, less than, less than or equal to	✓
<=> == === != =~ !~	Equality comparison (spaceship, equality, equality, not equal to, match, not match	✓ (not != or !~)

Table 2. Ruby's operators (continued)

Operator	Description	Method
&&	Logical *and*	
||	Logical *or*	
.. ...	Range inclusive, range exclusive	✓ (not ...)
? :	Ternary	
= += -= *= /= %= **= <<= >>= &= |= ^= &&= ||=	Assignment, abbreviated assignment	
not	Logical negation	
and or	Logical composition	
defined?	Special operator (no precedence)	

Comments

A comment hides a line, part of a line, or several lines from the Ruby interpreter. You can use the hash character (#) at the beginning of a line:

```
# I am a comment. Just ignore me.
```

Or, a comment may be on the same line after a statement or expression:

```
name = "Floydene" # ain't that a name to beat all
```

You can make a comment run over several lines, like this:

```
# This is a comment.
# This is a comment, too.
# This is a comment, too.
# I said that already.
```

Here is another form. This block comment conceals several lines from the interpreter with =begin/=end:

```
=begin
This is a comment.
This is a comment, too.
This is a comment, too.
I said that already.
=end
```

A block can comment out one line or as many lines as you want.

Numbers

Numbers are not primitives; each number is an object, an instance of one of Ruby's numeric classes. Numeric is Ruby's base class for numbers. The numeric class Fixnum is used for integers, fixed-length numbers with bit lengths of the native machine word, minus 1. The Float class is for floating-point numbers, which use the native architecture's double-precision floating-point representation internally. The Bignum class is used to hold integers larger than Fixnum can hold. Bignums are created automatically if any operation or assignment yields a result too large for Fixnum. The only limitation on the size integer Bignum can represent is the available memory in the operating system:

```
2411        # integer, of class Fixnum
2_411       # integer, of class Fixnum, underscore ignored
241.1       # float, of class Float
3.7e4       # scientific notation, of class Float
3E4         # scientific notation, of class Float
3E-4        # scientific notation, with sign before
            #   exponent
0444        # octal, of class Fixnum
0xfff       # hexadecimal, of class Fixnum
0b1101      # binary, of class Fixnum
4567832704  # integer, of class Bignum
```

Figure 1 shows a hierarchy of Ruby's math classes.

Variables

A *variable* is an identifier that is assigned to an object, and that object may hold a value. The type of the value is assigned at runtime. Ruby variables are not declared nor statically typed. Ruby uses *duck typing*, a kind of dynamic typing. If a value behaves or acts like a certain type, such as an integer, Ruby gives it a context, and it is treated in that context.

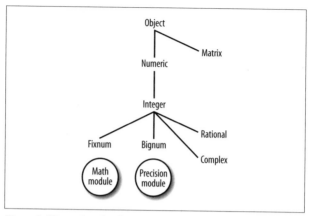

Figure 1. Hierarchy of Ruby math classes

Duck typing comes from the concept that if it walks like a duck, quacks like a duck, flies like a duck, and swims like a duck (or integer or float, etc.), then it is probably a duck. If a variable is able to act like an integer, for example, then it is legal to use it in that context.

Local Variables

A *local variable* has a local scope or context. For example, if a variable is defined inside of a method or a loop, its scope is within the method or loop where it was defined. Local variable names must start with a lowercase letter or with an underscore character (_), such as alpha or _beta, and cannot be prefixed with a special character (as in @, @@, or $).

Instance Variables

An *instance variable* belongs to a particular instance of a class (hence the name) and can only be accessed from outside that instance via an accessor (or helper) method. Instance variables are always prefixed with a single at sign (@), as in @hello. See the upcoming section "Classes."

Class Variables

A *class variable* is shared among all instances of a class. Only one copy of a class variable exists for a given class. In Ruby, it is prefixed by two at signs (@@), such as @@times. You have to initialize (declare a value for) a class variable before you use it. See the upcoming section "Classes."

Global Variables

Global variables are available globally to a program, inside any structure. Their scope is the whole program. They are prefixed by a dollar sign ($), such as $amount. Matz's opinion on global variables is, and I quote, "They are ugly, so don't use them." I would take his advice. You can use a singleton instead. See the upcoming section "Singletons."

Constants

Constant variable names must begin with a capital letter (Matz), and by convention are frequently all capitals (MATZ). This makes make them easy to spot. As their name suggests, constants are not expected to change their value after their initial assignment. Because Ruby is a flexible language, there are a couple of notable exceptions to this. First, you can reassign a constant in Ruby, though Ruby will generate a warning if you do, and it's not a good idea. Second, and more importantly, since constants refer to objects, the contents of the object *to which the constant refers* may change without Ruby generating a warning. Thus, Ruby constants are called *mutable*, because, although the constant is only expected to refer to a single object throughout the program, what's contained in that object may vary.

Parallel Assignment of Variables

With parallel assignment, you can assign several values to several variables in a single expression. A list of variables, separated by commas, can be placed to the left of the equals sign, with the list of values to assign them (in order) on the right. Here is an example:

```
x, y, z = 100, 200, 500
```

You can also assign values of different types:

```
a, b, c = "cash", 1.99, 100
```

Symbols

Ruby has a special object called a *symbol*. Symbols are like placeholders for identifiers and strings; they are always prefixed by a colon (:), such as :en and :logos. Most importantly, *only one copy* of the symbol is held in a single memory address, as long as the program is running. You don't directly create a symbol by assigning a value to one. You create a symbol by calling the to_sym or intern methods on a string, or by assigning a symbol to a symbol:

```
name = "Brianna"
name.to_sym # => :Brianna
:Brianna.id2name # => "Brianna"
name == :Brianna.id2name # => true
```

Predefined Variables

Table 3 lists all of Ruby's predefined variables.

Table 3. Predefined variables

Predefined variable	Description
$!	The exception information message containing the last exception raised. raise sets this variable. Access with => in a rescue clause.
$@	The stack backtrace of the last exception, retrievable via Exception#backtrace.
$&	The string matched by the last successful pattern match in this scope, or nil if the last pattern match failed. Same as m[0] where m is a MatchData object. Read only. Local.

Table 3. Predefined variables (continued)

Predefined variable	Description
$`	String preceding whatever was matched by the last successful pattern match in the current scope, or nil if the last pattern match failed. Same as m.pre_match where m is a MatchData object. Read only. Local.
$'	String following whatever was matched by the last successful pattern match in the current scope, or nil if the last pattern match failed. Same as m.post_match where m is a MatchData object. Read only. Local.
$+	Last bracket matched by the last successful search pattern, or nil if the last pattern match failed. Useful if you don't know which of a set of alternative patterns matched. Read only. Local.
$1, $2...	Subpattern from the corresponding set of parentheses in the last successful pattern matched, not counting patterns matched in nested blocks that have been exited already, or nil if the last pattern match failed. Same as m[n] where m is a MatchData object. Read only. Local.
$~	Information about the last match in the current scope. Regex#match returns the last match information. Setting this variable affects match variables like $&, $+, $1, $2, etc. The nth subexpression can be retrieved by $~[nth]. Local.
$=	Case-insensitive flag; nil by default.
$/	Input record separator, newline by default. Works like awk's RS variable. If it is set to nil, a whole file will be read at once. gets, readline, etc. take the input record separator as an optional argument.
$\	Output record separator for print and IO#write; nil by default.
$,	Output field separator between arguments; also the default separator for Array#join, which allows you to indicate a separator explicitly.
$;	The default separator for String#split; nil by default.
$.	The current input line number of the last file that was read. Same as ARGF.lineno.

Table 3. Predefined variables (continued)

Predefined variable	Description
$<	The virtual concatenation file of the files given by command-line arguments, or standard input (in case no argument file is supplied). $<.*filename* returns the current filename. Synonym for ARGF.
$>	Default output for print, printf, $stdout by default. Synonym for $defout.
$_	Last input line of string by gets or readline in the current scope; set to nil if gets or readline meets EOF. Local.
$0	Name of the current Ruby program being executed.
$*	Command-line arguments given for the script. The options for the Ruby interpreter are already removed.
$$	Process number (process.pid) of the Ruby program being executed.
$?	Exit status of the last executed process.
$:	Synonym for $LOAD_PATH.
$"	Array containing the module names loaded by require. Used for prevent require from loading modules twice.
$DEBUG	True if -d or --debug switch is set.
$defout	Default output for print, printf; $stdout by default. Synonym for $>.
$F	Receives output from split when -a specified. Set if -a is set along with -p and -n.
$FILENAME	Name of the file currently being read from ARGF. Same as ARGF.*filename* or $<.*filename*.
$LOAD_PATH	Synonym for $:.
$SAFE	Security level: *0* No checks on externally supplied (tainted) date. Default. *1* Potentially dangerous operations using tainted data are forbidden. *2* Potentially dangerous operations performed on processes and files are forbidden. *3* All newly created objects are considered tainted. *4* Modification of global data is forbidden.

Table 3. Predefined variables (continued)

Predefined variable	Description
$stdin	The current standard input; STDIN by default.
$stdout	The current standard output; STDOUT by default.
$stderr	The current standard error output; STDERR by default.
$VERBOSE	True if verbose flag is set by the -v, -w, or --verbose switch of the Ruby interpreter.
$-0	Alias of $/.
$-a	True if option -a is set. Read-only.
$-d	Alias of $DEBUG.
$-F	Alias of $;.
$-i	In in-place-edit mode, holds the extension, otherwise nil. Can enable or disable in-place-edit mode.
$-I	Alias of $:.
$-l	True if option -l is set. Read-only.
$-p	True if option -p is set. Read-only.

Pseudovariables

Table 4 shows Ruby's *pseudovariables*. A pseudovariable is an object that looks like a variable, acts like a constant, and can't be assigned a value. These are also listed in Table 1.

Table 4. Pseudovariables in Ruby

Pseudovariable	Description
false	Logical or Boolean false; instance of FalseClass.
nil	Empty, uninitialized, or invalid; always false, but not the same as zero; object of NilClass.
self	Current object (receiver invoked by a method).
true	Logical or Boolean true; instance of TrueClass.
__FILE__	Name of current source file.
__LINE__	Number of current line in the current source file.

Global Constants

Table 5 describes all of Ruby's global constants.

Table 5. Global constants

Constant	Description
ARGF	I/O-like stream that allows access to a virtual concatenation of all files provided on the command line, or standard input if no files are provided. Synonym for $<.
ARGV	Array that contains all the command-line arguments passed to a program. Synonym for $*.
DATA	An input stream for reading the lines of code following the __END__ directive. Not defined if __END__ is not present in code.
ENV	A hash-like object containing the program's environment variables; can be treated as a hash.
FALSE	Synonym for false; false is preferred.
NIL	Synonym for nil; nil is preferred.
PLATFORM	Synonym for RUBY_PLATFORM. Deprecated.
RELEASE_DATE	Synonym for RUBY_RELEASE_DATE. Deprecated.
RUBY_PLATFORM	A string indicating the platform of the Ruby interpreter; e.g., "powerpc-darwin8.9.0."
RUBY_RELEASE_DATE	A string indicating the release date of the Ruby interpreter; e.g., "2007-03-13."
RUBY_VERSION	The Ruby version; e.g., "1.8.6."
STDERR	Standard error output stream with default value of $stderr.
STDIN	Standard input stream with default value of $stdin.
STDOUT	Standard output stream with default value of $stdout.
TOPLEVEL_BINDING	A Binding object at Ruby's top level.
TRUE	Synonym for true; true is preferred.
VERSION	Synonym for RUBY_VERSION. Deprecated.

Ranges

Ruby supports ranges by means of the .. (inclusive) and ...
(exclusive) operators. For example, the range 1..12 includes
the numbers 1, 2, 3, 4, 5, 6, 7, 8, 9, 10, 11, 12, inclusive. However, in the range 1...12, the ending value 12 is excluded; in
other words, the effective numbers are 1, 2, 3, 4, 5, 6, 7, 8, 9,
10, 11.

The === method determines whether a value is a member of,
or included in a range:

```
(1..25) === 14 # => true, in range
(1..25) === 26 # => false, out of range
(1...25) === 25 # => false, out of range (... used)
```

You can use a range to do things like create an array of digits:

```
(1..9).to_a # => [1, 2, 3, 4, 5, 6, 7, 8, 9]
```

You can also create a range like this:

```
digits = Range.new(1, 9)
digits.to_a # => [1, 2, 3, 4, 5, 6, 7, 8, 9]
```

Methods

Methods provide a way to collect programming statements
and expressions into one place so that you can use them con-
veniently and, if necessary, repeatedly. Most of the operators
in Ruby are actually methods. Here is a simple definition of a
method named hello, created with the keywords def and
end:

```
def hello
  puts "Hello, world!"
end

hello # => Hello, world!
```

You can undefine a method with undef:

```
undef hello # undefines the method named hello
```

```
hello # try calling this method now
NameError: undefined local variable or method `hello' for
main:Object
        from (irb):11
        from :0
```

Methods can take arguments. The repeat method shown here takes two arguments, word and times:

```
def repeat( word, times )
 puts word * times
end
```

```
repeat("Hello! ", 3) # => Hello! Hello! Hello!
repeat "Goodbye! ", 4 # => Goodbye! Goodbye! Goodbye!
Goodbye!
```

Parentheses

Parentheses are optional in most Ruby method definitions and calls. If you don't use parentheses when calling a method that takes arguments, you may get warnings, depending on the argument types.

Return Values

Methods have return values. In other languages, you explicitly return a value with a return statement. In Ruby, the value of the last expression evaluated is returned, *with or without* an explicit return statement. This is a Ruby idiom. You can also define a return value explicitly with the return keyword:

```
def hello
  return "Hello, world!"
end
```

Method Name Conventions

Ruby has conventions about the last character in method names—conventions that are very common but not enforced by the language. If a method name ends with a question mark (?), such as eql?, it means that the method returns a Boolean—true or false. For example:

```
x = 1.0
y = 1.0
x.eql? y # => true
```

If a method name ends in an exclamation point (!), like delete!, it indicates that the method is destructive, meaning it makes *in-place* changes to an object, rather than to a copy; that is, it changes the object itself. See the difference in the result of the String methods delete and delete!:

```
der_mensch = "Matz!" # => "Matz!"
der_mensch.delete( "!" ) # => "Matz"
puts der_mensch # => Matz!
der_mensch.delete!( "!" ) # => "Matz"
puts der_mensch # => Matz
```

If a method name ends in an equals sign (=), in the form family_name=, it means that the method is a setter—one that performs an assignment to, or sets a variable such as an instance variable in, a class:

```
class Name
  def family_name=( family )
    @family_name = family
  end
  def given_name=( given )
    @given_name = given
  end
end

n = Name.new
n.family_name= "Matsumoto" # => "Matsumoto"
n.given_name= "Yukihiro" # => "Yukihiro"
p n # => <Name:0x1d441c @family_name="Matsumoto", @given_name="Yukihiro">
```

Default Arguments

The repeat method shown earlier has two arguments. You can give those arguments default values by using an equals sign followed by a value. When you call the method without arguments, the defaults are used automatically. Redefine repeat with default values: Hello for word, and 3 for times. Call it first without arguments, then with them.

```ruby
def repeat( word="Hello! ", times=3 )
 puts word * times
end

repeat # => Hello! Hello! Hello!

repeat( "Goodbye! ", 5 ) # => Goodbye! Goodbye! Goodbye!
Goodbye! Goodbye!
```

Variable Arguments

You can be flexible about the number of arguments that a method has, because Ruby lets you pass a variable number of arguments by prefixing an argument with a splat (*):

```ruby
def num_args( *args )
  length = args.size
  label = length == 1 ? " argument" : " arguments"
  num = length.to_s + label + " ( " + args.inspect + " )"
  num
end

puts num_args # => 0 arguments ( [] )

puts num_args(1) # => 1 argument ( [1] )

puts num_args( 100, 2.5, "three" )
# => 3 arguments ( [100, 2.5, "three"] )
```

You can have set arguments along with variable arguments:

```ruby
def two_plus( one, two, *args )
  length = args.size
  label = length == 1 ? " variable argument" : " variable
arguments"
```

```
  num = length.to_s + label + " (" + args.inspect + ")"
  num
end

puts two_plus( 1, 2 ) # => 0 variable arguments ( [] )

puts two_plus( 1000, 3.5, 14.3 )
# => 1 variable argument ( [14.3] )

puts two_plus( 100, 2.5, "three", 70, 14.3 )
# => 3 variable arguments ( ["three", 70, 14.3] )
```

Aliasing Methods

Ruby has a keyword, alias, that creates method aliases. *Aliasing* means that you in effect create a copy of the method with a new method name, though both method invocations will point to the same object. The following example illustrates how to create an alias for the method greet:

```
def greet
  puts "Hello, baby!"
end

alias baby greet # alias greet as baby

greet # call it
Hello, baby!

baby # call the aliased version
Hello, baby!
```

Blocks

A *block* in Ruby is more than just a code block or group of statements. A Ruby block is always invoked in conjunction with a method, as you will see. In fact, blocks are closures, sometimes referred to as *nameless functions*. They are like a method within another method that refers to or shares variables with the enclosing or outer method. In Ruby, the closure or block is wrapped by braces ({}) or by do/end, and depends on the associated method (such as each) to work.

Here is an example call to a block on the method each from Array:

```
pacific = [ "Washington", "Oregon", "California" ]

pacific.each do |element|
  puts element
end
```

The name in the bars (|element|) can be any name you want. The block uses it as a local variable to keep track of every element in the array, and later uses it to do something with the element. You can replace do/end with a pair of braces, as is most commonly done. The braces actually have a higher precedence than do/end:

```
pacific.each { |e| puts e }
```

If you use a variable name that already exists in the containing scope, the block assigns that variable each successive value, which may or may not be what you want. It does not generate a local variable to the block with that name, as some might expect. Thus, you get this behavior:

```
j = 7
(1..4).to_a.each { | j | } #  j now equals 4
```

The yield statement

A yield statement executes a block associated with a method. For example, this gimme method contains nothing more than a yield statement:

```
def gimme
  yield
end
```

To find out what yield does, call gimme and see what happens:

```
gimme
LocalJumpError: no block given
        from (irb):11:in `gimme'
        from (irb):13
        from :0
```

You get an error here because yield's job is to execute the code block that is associated with the method. That was missing in the call to gimme. We can avoid this error by using the block_given? method (from Kernel). Redefine gimme with an if statement:

```
def gimme
  if block_given?
    yield
  else
    puts "I'm blockless!"
  end
end
```

Try again with and without a block:

```
gimme { print "Say hi to the people." } # => Say hi to the
people.

gimme # => I'm blockless!
```

Redefine gimme to contain two yields, then call it with a block:

```
def gimme
  if block_given?
    yield
    yield
  else
    puts "I'm blockless!"
  end
end

gimme { print "Say hi again. " } # => Say hi again. Say hi
again.
```

Another thing you should know is that after yield executes, control comes back to the next statement immediately following yield.

Procs

Ruby lets you store procedures—or procs—as objects, complete with their context. You can do this several ways. You can create a proc with new on the Proc class or by calling either the lambda or proc method from Kernel. Calling lambda or proc is preferred over Proc.new because lambda and proc do parameter checking. Consider this example:

```
count = Proc.new { [1,2,3,4,5].each do |i| print i end;
puts }
your_proc = lambda { puts "Lurch: 'You rang?'" }
my_proc = proc { puts "Morticia: 'Who was at the door,
Lurch?'" }

# What kind of objects did you just create?
puts count.class, your_proc.class, my_proc.class

# Calling all procs
count.call # => 12345
your_proc.call # => Lurch: 'You rang?'
my_proc.call # => Morticia: 'Who was at the door, Lurch?'
```

You can convert a block passed as a method argument to a Proc object by preceding the argument name with an ampersand (&) as follows:

```
def return_block
  yield
end

def return_proc( &proc )
  yield
end

return_block { puts "Got block!" }
return_proc { puts "Got block, convert to proc!" }
```

The method return_block has no arguments. All it has is a yield statement in its body. The yield statement's purpose, once again, is to execute a block when the block is passed to a method. The next method, return_proc, has one argument, &proc. When a method has an argument preceded by an ampersand, it accepts the block, when one is submitted, and converts it to a Proc object. With yield in the body, the method executes the block *cum* proc, without having to bother with the Proc call method.

Conditional Statements

A conditional statement tests whether a statement is true or false and performs logic based on the answer. Both true and false are pseudovariables—you can't assign values to them. The former is an object of TrueClass, and the latter is an object of FalseClass.

The if Statement

These statements begin with if and close with end:

```
if x == y then puts "x equals y" end

if x != y: puts "x is not equal to y" end

if x > y
  puts "x is greater than y"
end
```

The separator then (or its synonym :) is optional unless the statement is on one line.

Negation

The negation operator ! reverses the true/false value of its expression:

```
if !x == y then puts "x does not equal y" end

if !x > y
  puts "x is not greater than y"
end
```

Multiple tests

Combine multiple tests in an if statement using && and ||, or their synonyms and and or, which have lower precedence:

```
ruby = "nifty"
programming = "fun"

if ruby == "nifty" && programming == "fun"
  puts "Keep programming!"
end
```

```
if a == 10 && b == 27 && c == 43 && d == -14
  print sum = a + b + c + d
end

if ruby=="nifty" and programming=="fun" and
weather=="nice"
  puts "Stop programming and go outside for a break!"
end

if a == 10 || b == 27 || c = 43 || d = -14
  print sum = a + b + c + d
end

if ruby == "nifty" or programming == "fun"
  puts "Keep programming!"
end
```

Statement modifier for if

You can also use if as a statement modifier by placing the if
at the end of the statement:

```
puts "x is less than y" if x < y
```

The else statement

Add an optional else to execute a statement when if is not
true:

```
if x >= y
  puts "x greater than or equal to y"
else
  puts "x is not greater than or equal to y"
end
```

The elsif statement

Use one or more optional elsif statements to test multiple
statements (ending with an optional else—it must be last):

```
if x == y
  puts "x equals y"
elsif x != y
  puts "x is not equal to y"
elsif x > y
  puts "x is greater than y"
```

```
  elsif x < y
    puts "x is less than y"
  elsif x >= y
    puts "x is greater than or equal to y"
  elsif x <= y
    puts "x is less than or equal to y"
  else
    puts "Arrrrgh!"
  end
```

Here is a tighter way of using elsifs with a colon after each test:

```
lang = "de"

if lang == "en": print "dog"
  elsif lang == "es": print "perro"
  elsif lang == "fr": print "chien"
  elsif lang == "de": print "Hund"
  else puts "No language set; default = 'dog'".
  end
```

Don't follow the else (the last statement) with a colon.

The unless Statement

An unless statement is a negated form of the if statement. This example of unless:

```
unless lang == "de"
  dog = "dog"
else
  dog = "Hund"
end
```

is a negated form of this if statement (both accomplish the same thing):

```
if lang == "de"
  dog = "Hund"
else
  dog = "dog"
end
```

This example is saying, in effect, that unless the *value* of lang is de, dog will be assigned the value of dog; otherwise, assign dog the value Hund.

Statement modifier for unless

As with if, you can also use unless as a statement modifier:

```ruby
puts num += 1 unless num > 88
```

The while Statement

A while loop executes the code it contains as long as its conditional statement remains true:

```ruby
i = 0
breeds = [ "quarter", "arabian", "appalosa", "paint" ]
puts breeds.size # => 4
temp = []

while i < breeds.size do
  temp << breeds[i].capitalize
  i +=1
end

temp.sort! # => ["Appalosa", "Arabian", "Paint",
"Quarter"]
breeds.replace( temp )
p breeds # => ["Appalosa", "Arabian", "Paint", "Quarter"]
```

The do keyword is optional:

Another form of while you can use is with begin and end, where the code in the loop is evaluated before the conditional is checked (like do/while in C):

```ruby
temp = 98.3

begin
  print "Your temperature is " + temp.to_s + " Fahrenheit. "
  puts "I think you're okay."
  temp += 0.1
end while temp < 98.6

puts "Your temperature is " + temp.to_s + " Fahrenheit."
```

You can break out of a while loop with the keyword break:

```ruby
while i < breeds.size
  temp << breeds[i].capitalize
  break if temp[i] == "Arabian"
```

```
    i +=1
  end
  p temp # => ["Quarter", "Arabian"]
```

When the if modifier following break found Arabian in the temp array, it broke out of the loop right then.

Statement modifier for while

As with if, you can use while as a statement modifier, at the end of a statement:

```
cash = 100_000.00
sum = 0

cash += 1.00, sum while cash < 1_000_000.00 # underscore
ignored
```

The until Statement

As unless is a negated form of if, until is a negated form of while. Compare the following statements:

```
weight = 150
while weight < 200 do
  puts "Weight: " + weight.to_s
  weight += 5
end
```

Here is the same logic expressed with until:

```
weight = 150
until weight == 200 do
  puts "Weight: " + weight.to_s
  weight += 5
end
```

And as with while, you have another form you can use with until, that is, with begin/end:

```
weight = 150

begin
  puts "Weight: " + weight.to_s
  weight += 5
end until weight == 200
```

In this form, the statements in the loop are evaluated once before the conditional is checked.

Statement modifier for until

And finally, like while, you can also use until as a statement modifier:

```
puts age += 1 until age > 28
```

The case Statement

Ruby's case statement together with when provides a way to express conditional logic in a succinct way. It is similar to the switch statement found in other languages, but case can check objects of any type that can respond to the equality property and/or any equivalence operators, including strings. Using case/when is more convenient and concise than if/elsif/else because the logic of == is assumed. Examples follow:

```
lang = "fr"

dog = case lang
  when "en": "dog"
  when "es": "perro"
  when "fr": "chien"
  when "de": "Hund"
  else       "dog"
end
```

The string chien is assigned to the variable dog because the value of lang is the symbol fr. If the lang variable held a symbol instead of a string, the code would look like:

```
lang = :de

dog = case lang
  when :en: "dog"
  when :es: "perro"
  when :fr: "chien"
  when :de: "Hund"
  else      "dog"
end
```

The string value Hund is assigned to dog because the value of lang is :de. The next example uses several ranges to test values.

```
scale = 8
case scale
  when     0: puts "lowest"
  when 1..3: puts "medium-low"
  when 4..5: puts "medium"
  when 6..7: puts "medium-high"
  when 8..9: puts "high"
  when    10: puts "highest"
  else        puts "off scale"
end
```

The printed response will be high because scale is in the range 8 to 9, inclusive.

The for Loop

This example of a for loop uses a range (1..10) to print out a list of numbers from 1 to 10, inclusive. The do is optional, unless the for loop is on one line:

```
for i in 1..10 do print i, " " end # => 1 2 3 4 5 6 7 8 9 10

for i in 1..10
  print i, " "
end
# => 1 2 3 4 5 6 7 8 9 10
```

This for loop prints out a times table (from 1 to 12) for the number 2:

```
for i in 1..12
  print "2 x " + i.to_s + " = ", i * 2, "\n"
end
```

This is a nested for loop that you can use to print times tables from 1 times to 12 times:

```
for i in 1..12
  for j in 1..12
    print i.to_s + " x " + j.to_s + " = ", j * i, "\n"
  end
end
```

An alternative to the for loop is the times method (from class Integer):

```
12.times { |i| print i, " " } # => 0 1 2 3 4 5 6 7 8 9 10 11
```

The Ternary Operator

The ternary or base three operator (?:) is a concise structure that descended from C to Ruby. It is also called the *conditional expression*. An example follows:

```
label = length == 1 ? " argument" : " arguments"
```

This expression assigns a string value to label based on the value of length. If the value of length is 1, the string value argument (singular) will be assigned to label; but if it is not true—that is, length has a value other than 1—the string value of label will be arguments (plural).

Executing Code Before or After a Program

The following structures allow code to execute *before* and *after* a program runs. Both BEGIN and END are followed by blocks enclosed by braces ({}):

```
BEGIN { puts "Date and time: " + Time.now.to_s }

def bmi( weight, height )
  703.0*( weight.to_f/(height.to_f**2))
end

my_bmi = bmi( 196, 73 )

puts "Your BMI is: " + x = sprintf( "%0.2f", my_bmi )

END { puts "You've got some work ahead of you." }
```

Classes

In an object-oriented programming language like Ruby, a *class* is a container that holds properties (class members) such as methods and variables. Classes can inherit properties from a parent or superclass, creating a hierarchy of classes with a base class at the root or top. In Ruby, the base class is Object. Ruby uses single inheritance—that is, a Ruby class can inherit the properties of only one parent class. (Multiple inheritance, as is used in C++, allows a class to inherit from more than one parent.) You can define more than one class in a single file in Ruby. A class itself is an object, even if you don't directly instantiate it. Classes are always open, so you can add to any class, even a built-in one.

A class is defined with a class keyword, and the definition concludes with an end:

```ruby
class Hello

  def initialize( name )
    @name = name
  end

  def hello_matz
    puts "Hello, " + @name + "!"
  end

end

hi = Hello.new( "Matz" )
hi.hello_matz # => Hello, Matz!
```

The initialize method defines the instance variable @name by storing a copy of the name argument passed into the initialize method. The initialize method is a Ruby convention that acts like a class constructor in other languages, but not completely. At this point, the instance is already there, fully instantiated. initialize is the first code that is executed *after* the object is instantiated; you can execute just about any Ruby code in initialize. initialize is always private; that is, it is scoped only to the current object, not beyond it. You access the instance variable @name with the method hello_matz.

To add a method to an existing class, such as the built-in class Array, specify the following:

```
class Array

  def array_of_ten
    (1..10).to_a
  end

end

arr = Array.new
ten = arr.array_of_ten
p ten # => [1, 2, 3, 4, 5, 6, 7, 8, 9, 10]
```

Instance Variables

As mentioned previously, an *instance variable* is a variable
that is available from within an instance of a class, and is lim-
ited in scope because it belongs to a given object. An instance
variable is prefixed by a single at sign (@), like:

```
@name = "Easy Jet"
```

You can define an instance variable inside a method or outside of one. You can only access an instance variable from
outside an object via a method. You can, however, access an
instance variable *within* the object without a method:

```
class Horse

  @name = "Easy Jet"

end
```

This works if you only want to reference @name from within
the object. You have no way to retrieve the value of @name
directly from outside of the object. You must define a getter
(accessor) method to retrieve the value:

```
class Horse

  def name
    @name = "Easy Jet"
  end

end
```

```
h = Horse.new
h.name # => "Easy Jet"
```

You often want a setter in addition to a getter. A *setter* is an accessor method that sets the value of a variable:

```
class Horse

  def name
    @name
  end

  def name=( value )
    @name = value
  end

end

h = Horse.new
h.name= "Poco Bueno"
h.name # => "Poco Bueno"
```

The setter method name= follows a Ruby convention: the name of the method ends with an equals sign (=). This convention is not a requirement. You could call name= whatever you like, as long as the characters are legal. Here is another version of the class Horse that initializes the instance variable @name with the standard initialize method. Later the program creates an instance of the class by calling new, and then accesses the instance variable through the accessor method horse_name, via the instance horse:

```
class Horse

  def initialize( name )
    @name = name
  end

  def horse_name
    @name
  end

end

horse = Horse.new( "Doc Bar" )
puts horse.horse_name # => Doc Bar
```

Accessors

Ruby simplifies the creation of getters and setters by meta-programming with the methods attr, attr_reader, attr_writer, and attr_accessor, all from the Module class. The attr method creates a single getter method, named by a symbol, with an optional setter method (if the second argument is true):

```ruby
class Dog
  attr :bark, true
end

Dog.instance_methods - Object.instance_methods
# => ["bark", "bark="]

dog = Dog.new

dog.bark="Woof!"
puts dog.bark # => Woof!
```

By calling attr with :bark and true as arguments, the class Dog will have the instance methods bark and bark=. If you call attr with only the :bark argument, Dog would have only the getter method bark. (Notice that you can subtract out Object's instance methods with - when retrieving Dog's instance methods.)

The attr_reader and attr_writer methods accept as arguments the names of one or more instance variables, then create corresponding methods that return (attr_reader) or set (attr_writer) the values of each instance variable. (Instance variables are not actually created until you assign values to them.) Consider this example:

```ruby
class Dog
  attr_reader :bark # getter
  attr_writer :bark # setter
end

dog = Dog.new

dog.bark="Woof!"
puts dog.bark # => Woof!
```

```
dog.instance_variables.sort # => ["@bark"]
Dog.instance_methods.sort - Object.instance_methods
# => [ "bark", "bark=" ]
```

Calling the attr_accessor method does the same job as calling both attr_reader and attr_writer together, for one or more instance variables:

```
class Gaits
  attr_accessor :walk, :trot, :canter
end

Gaits.instance_methods.sort - Object.instance_methods # =>
["canter", "canter=", "trot", "trot=", "walk", "walk="]
```

Class Variables

A *class variable* is shared among all instances of a class, so only one copy of a class variable exists for a given class. In Ruby, a class variable is prefixed by two at signs (@@). You *must* initialize a class attribute before you use it, such as @@times = 0.

```
class Repeat
  @@total = 0
  def initialize( string, times )
    @string = string
    @times = times
  end
  def repeat
    @@total += @times
    return @string * @times
  end
  def total
    "Total times, so far: " + @@total.to_s
  end
end

data = Repeat.new( "ack ", 8 )
ditto = Repeat.new( "Again! ", 5 )
ditty = Repeat.new( "Rinse. Lather. Repeat. ", 2 )

puts data.repeat # => ack ack ack ack ack ack ack ack
puts data.total # => Total times, so far: 8
```

```
puts ditto.repeat # => Again! Again! Again! Again! Again!
puts ditto.total # => Total times, so far: 13

puts ditty.repeat
# => Rinse. Lather. Repeat. Rinse. Lather. Repeat.
puts ditty.total # => Total times, so far: 15
```

Class Methods

A *class method* is a method that is associated with a class
(and with a module in Ruby), not an instance of a class. You
can invoke class methods by prefixing the name of the
method with the name of the class to which it belongs, such
as to Math.sqrt(36). Class methods are also called *static
methods*. You can also associate the name of a module with a
method name, just like with a class, but to use such a method,
you must include the module in a class. To define a class
method, you simply prefix the name of the method with the
name of the class or module (or self) in the method definition:

```
class Area

# Use self.rect or Area.rect
# def self.rect( length, width, units="inches" )
  def Area.rect( length, width, units="inches" )
    area = length*width
    printf( "The area of this rectangle is %.2f %s.",
              area, units )
    sprintf( "%.2f", area )
  end

end

Area.rect(12.5, 16) # => The area of this rectangle is
200.00 inches.
```

Singletons

Another way you can define class methods is by using a class
within a class and self—a *singleton* class. In basic terms, a
singleton is designed so that it can only be instantiated once.

It is often used like a global variable. Ruby has a class for defining singleton objects; see *http://www.ruby-doc.org/core/classes/Singleton.html*. Consider this example:

```ruby
class Area

  class << self

    def rect( length, width, units="inches" )
      area = length*width
      printf( "The area of this rectangle is %.2f %s.",
                   area, units )
      sprintf( "%.2f", area )
    end

  end

end

Area.rect(10, 10) # The area of this rectangle is 100.00
inches.=> "100.00"
```

In this form, you don't have to prefix the method with the class name. A singleton class is tied to a particular object, can be instantiated only once, and is not distinguished by a prefixed name. The method rect is also effectively a *singleton method* because it is tied to the singleton class. Here is a way to define a singleton method, one that is tied to a single object:

```ruby
class Singleton
end

s = Singleton.new
def s.handle
  puts "I'm a singleton method!"
end

s.handle # => I'm a singleton method!
```

Inheritance

As mentioned earlier, when a child class inherits or derives from a parent, it has access to the methods and properties of the parent class. Inheritance is accomplished with the < operator:

```
class Name

  attr_accessor :given_name, :family_name

end

class Address < Name

  attr_accessor :street, :city, :state, :country

end

a = Address.new
puts a.respond_to?(:given_name) # => true
```

If the class Name were in a different file, you'd just require that file first, and then the inheritance operation works.

Load path

The system path is not necessarily the same thing as the Ruby path or load path. Ruby has a predefined variable called $LOAD_PATH (which also has a Perl-like synonym, $:). $LOAD_PATH is an array that contains the names of directories that are searched by load and require methods when loading files. Ruby can also use the environment variables PATH and RUBYPATH (if they are set). PATH is the system path and acts as a search path for Ruby programs, among other things; RUBYPATH may be the same thing as PATH, but because it takes precedence over PATH, it is likely to hold other directories beyond it.

Public, Private, or Protected

The visibility or access of methods and constants may be set with the following methods:

public
> The method is accessible by anyone from anywhere; this is the default.

private
> The receiver for the method is always the current object or self, so its scope is always the current object (often helper methods; that is, ones that get called by other methods to perform some job).

protected
> The method can be used only by instances of the class where it was defined, or by derived classes.

Methods following the keywords private or protected will have the indicated visibility, until changed or until the definition ends:

```ruby
class Names

  def initialize( given, family, nick, pet )
    @given = given
    @family = family
    @nick = nick
    @pet = pet
  end

  # the methods are public by default

  def given
    @given
  end

  def family
    @family
  end

  # all following methods private, until changed

  private

  def nick
    @nick
  end
```

```
# all following methods protected, until changed

  protected

  def pet
    @pet
  end

end

name = Names.new( "Klyde", "Kimball", "Abner", "Teddy
Bear" )

name.given # => "Klyde"
name.family # => "Kimball"

# see what happens when you call nick or pet

name.nick
name.pet
```

You can also call the methods after a definition (you must
use symbols for method names):

```
def pet
  @pet
end

protected :pet
```

Modules and Mixins

In addition to classes, Ruby also has modules. A module is
like a class, but it cannot be instantiated like a class. A class
can *include* a module so that when the class is instantiated, it
gets the included module's methods and so forth. (The
include method comes from the Module class: *http://www.
ruby-doc.org/core/classes/Module.html*.) The methods from
an included module become instance methods in the class
that includes the module. This is called *mixing in*, and a
module is referred to as a *mixin*. You can include more than

one module (which is similar to multiple inheritance), but you can only inherit from one class (single inheritance). Because identifiers are overridden by the last definition of the identifier (e.g., for methods or constants), this scheme avoids name collision. A module is a form of a namespace in Ruby. A *namespace* is a set of names—such as method names—that have a scope or context. A Ruby class can also be considered a namespace.

A Ruby module associates a single name with a set of method and constant names. The module name can be used in classes or in other modules. Generally, the scope or context of such a namespace is the class or module where the namespace (module name) is included.

A module name must be a constant; that is, it must start with an uppercase letter. A module can contain methods, constants, other modules, and even classes. It can inherit from another module, but it may not inherit from a class. As a class may include a module, it may also include modules that have inherited other modules. Here's an example:

```
module Dice

  # virtual roll of a pair of dice
  def roll
    r_1 = rand(6); r_2 = rand(6)
    r1 = r_1>0?r_1:1; r2 = r_2>0?r_2:6
    total = r1+r2
    printf( "You rolled %d and %d (%d).\n", r1, r2, total )
    total
  end

end

class Game
 include Dice
end

g = Game.new
g.roll
```

If the module Dice and the class Game were in separate files, just require the file containing the module before including the module. The file containing the Dice module might look like this:

```
module Dice

  # virtual roll of a pair of dice
  def roll
    r_1 = rand(6); r_2 = rand(6)
    r1 = r_1>0?r_1:1; r2 = r_2>0?r_2:6
    total = r1+r2
    printf( "You rolled %d and %d (%d).\n", r1, r2, total )
    total
  end

end
```

And the file containing the Game class might look like this:

```
#!/usr/bin/env ruby

require 'dice'

class Game
 include Dice
end

g = Game.new
g.roll
```

When you define module methods like class methods—that is, prefixed with the module name (or with self)—you can call the method as shown here:

```
module Binary

# def self.to_bin( num )
  def Binary.to_bin( num )
    bin = sprintf("%08b", num)
  end

end

Binary.to_bin( 123 ) # => "01111011"
```

Files

You can manipulate file directories (folders) and files from within Ruby programs using methods from the Dir and File classes. For documentation, see *http://www.ruby-doc.org/core/classes/Dir.html* and *http://www.ruby-doc.org/core/classes/File.html*. For example, you can change directories (using an absolute path), and then store the value of the directory path in a variable as follows:

```
Dir.chdir( "/Users/penelope" )
home = Dir.pwd # => "/Users/penelope/"
p home # => "/Users/penelope"
```

If you need a directory, create it with mkdir; later on, delete it with rmdir (or delete, a synonym of rmdir):

```
Dir.mkdir( "/Users/herman/sandbox" )
Dir.rmdir( "/Users/herman/sandbox" )
```

You can also set permissions (where the mask 755 sets permissions owner, group, world [anyone] to rwxr-xr-x where r = read, w = write, and x = execute) on a new directory (not one that already exists) with mkdir:

```
Dir.mkdir( "/Users/floyd/sandbox", 755 )
```

Creating a New File

To create a new file and open it at the same time, use the File method new, like this:

```
file = File.new( "file.rb", "w" )
```

The first argument names the new file, and the second argument specifies the file mode, either r for readable, w for writable, or x for executable. The effects of the different modes are shown in Table 6.

Table 6. File modes

Mode	Description
"r"	Read-only, starts at beginning of file (default mode).
"r+"	Read-write, starts at beginning of file.
"w"	Write-only, truncates existing file to zero length or creates a new file for writing.
"w+"	Read-write, truncates existing file to zero length or creates a new file for reading and writing.
"a"	Write-only, starts at end of file if file exists, otherwise creates a new file for writing.
"a+"	Read-write, starts at end of file if file exists, otherwise creates a new file for reading and writing.
"b"	(DOS/Windows only) Binary file mode (may appear with any of the key letters listed above).

Opening an Existing File

You open an existing file with the open method. Use file.closed? to test whether a file is closed. It returns true or false:

```
file = File.open( "my_text.txt" )
file.each { |line| print "#{file.lineno}. ", line }
file.closed?  # => false
file.close
```

The expression substitution syntax—that is, #{file.lineno}, inserts the line number in the output, followed by the line from the file. The open, each, and close methods are all from the IO class, not File.

ARGV and ARGF

Another interesting way to output the contents of a file is with ARGV, using only two lines of code:

```
ARGV << "my_text.txt"
print while gets
```

ARGV (or $*) is an array, and each of its elements is a file-name submitted on the command line, usually. But in this case, we have appended a filename to ARGV directly with <<, an array method. You can apply any method to ARGV that you might apply to any other array. For example, try adding this command:

```
p ARGV
```

Or:

```
p ARGV#[0]
```

The gets method is a Kernel method that gets lines from ARGV, and as long as gets returns a string, that line is printed with print.

ARGF ($<) is, once again, a virtual concatenation of all the files that appear on the command line:

```
while line = ARGF.gets
  print line
end
```

While there is a line to be retrieved from files on the command line, the code prints that line to standard output. To see how it works, run the program with several files on the command line:

```
argf.rb my_text.txt my_text_2.txt
```

Both files (if they existed) are printed on the display, one line at a time.

Renaming and Deleting Files

You can rename and delete files programmatically with Ruby with the rename and delete methods. Type these lines into *irb*:

```
File.new( "to_do.txt", "w" )

File.rename( "to_do.txt", "chaps.txt" )

File.delete( "chaps.txt" )
```

File Inquiries

The following command tests whether a file exists before opening it:

```
File.open("file.rb") if File::exists?( "file.rb" )
```

exist? (singular) is a synonym of exists?.

Inquire whether the file is really a file with file?:

```
File.file?( "my_text.txt" ) # => true
```

Or find out if it is a directory with directory?:

```
# a directory
File::directory?( "/usr/local/bin" ) # => true

# a file
File::directory?( "file.rb" ) # => false
```

Test whether the file is readable with readable?, writable with writable?, and executable with executable?:

```
File.readable?( "mumble.txt" ) # => true
File.writable?( "bumble.txt" ) # => true
File.executable?( "rumble.txt" ) # => false
```

You can find out if a file has a length of zero (0) with zero?:

```
system("touch blurb.txt") # Create a zero-length file
File.zero?( "blurb.txt" ) # => true
```

Get its size in bytes with size? or size:

```
File.size?( "sonnet_129.txt" ) # => 594
File.size( "sonnet_129.txt" ) # => 594
```

size is a synonym for size?.

Finally, inquire about the type of a file with ftype:

```
File::ftype( "file.rb" ) # => "file"
```

The ftype method identifies the type of the file by returning one of the following: file, directory, characterSpecial, blockSpecial, fifo, link, socket, or unknown.

Find out when a file was created, modified, or last accessed with ctime, mtime, and atime, respectively:

```
File::ctime( "file.rb" ) # => Wed May 08 10:06:37 -0700
2007
File::mtime( "file.rb" ) # => Wed May 08 10:44:44 -0700
2007
File::atime( "file.rb" ) # => Wed May 08 10:45:01 -0700
2007
```

File Modes and Ownership

Use the chmod method with a mask (see Table 7) to change the mode or permissions/access list of a file:

```
file = File.new( "to_do.txt", "w" )
file.chmod( 0755 )
```

Another method:

```
file = File.new( "to_do.txt", "w" ).chmod( 0755 )
system "ls -l"
# => -rwxr-xr-x   1 ralphy  techw   0 May  8 22:13 to_do.txt
```

This means that only the owner can write the file, but anyone can read or execute it. Compare:

```
file = File.new( "to_do.txt", "w" ).chmod( 0644 )
system "ls -l"
# => -rw-r--r--   1 ralphy  techw   0 May  8 22:13 to_do.txt
```

Everyone can read the file, but only the owner can write the file, and no one can execute it.

Table 7. Masks for chmod

Mask	Description
0700	rwx mask for owner
0400	r for owner
0200	w for owner
0100	x for owner
0070	rwx mask for group
0040	r for group

Table 7. Masks for chmod (continued)

Mask	Description
0020	w for group
0010	x for group
0007	rwx mask for other
0004	r for other
0002	w for other
0001	x for other
4000	Set user ID on execution
2000	Set group ID on execution
1000	Save swapped text, even after use

You can change the owner and group of a file with the chown method, which is like the Unix/Linux command chown (you need superuser or root privileges to use this method):

```
file = File.new( "to_do.txt", "r" )
file.chown( 109, 3333 )
```

Or:

```
file = File.new( "to_do.txt", "r" ).chown( 109, 3333 )
```

Now perform this system command (works on Unix/Linux systems only) to see the result:

```
system "ls -l to_do.txt"
# => -rw-r--r--   1 109  3333  0 Nov  8 11:38 to_do.txt
```

The IO Class

The basis for all input and output in Ruby is the IO class, which represents an input/output (I/O) stream of data in the form of bytes. Standard streams include standard input stream ($stdin) or the keyboard; standard output stream ($stdout), the display or screen; and standard error output stream ($stderr), which is also the display by default. IO is closely associated with the File class, and File is the only standard subclass of IO in Ruby. I'll show you a sampling of IO code.

To create a new I/O stream named ios, use the new method. The first argument is 1 which is the *numeric file descriptor* for standard input. Standard input can also be represented by the predefined Ruby variable $stdin (see Table 8). The optional second argument, w, is a mode string meaning *write*:

```ruby
ios = IO.new( 1, "w" )

ios.puts "IO, IO, it's off to the computer lab I go."

$stdout.puts "Do you copy?"
```

Table 8. Standard streams

Stream description	File descriptor	Predefined Ruby variable	Ruby environment variable
Standard input stream	0	$stdin	STDIN
Standard output stream	1	$stdout	STDOUT
Standard error output stream	2	$stderr	STDERR

Other mode strings include r or read-only (the default), r+ for read-write, and w for write-only. For details on all available modes, see Table 9.

Table 9. I/O modes

Mode	Description
r	Read-only. Starts at the beginning of the file (default mode).
r+	Read-write. Starts at the beginning of the file.
w	Write-only. Truncates existing file to zero length, or creates a new file for writing.
w+	Read-write. Truncates existing file to zero length, or creates a new file for reading and writing.
a	Write-only. Starts at the end of file, if the file exists; otherwise, creates a new file for writing.
a+	Read-write, starts at the end of the file, if file exists; otherwise, creates a new file for reading and writing.
b	Binary file mode. May appear with any of the modes listed in this table. DOS/Windows only.

With the IO instance method `fileno`, you can test what the numeric file descriptor is for your I/O stream (`to_i` also works):

```
ios.fileno # => 1
ios.to_i # => 1

$stdout.fileno # => 1
```

You can also write strings to the stream (buffer) with the `<<` method, then flush the buffer with `flush`:

```
ios << "Ask not " << "for whom the bell tolls." << " -John
Donne"

ios.flush # => Ask not for whom the bell tolls. -John
Donne
```

Finally, close the stream with close (this also flushes any pending writes):

```
ios.close
```

Exception Handling

Exceptions occur when a program gets off course, and the normal program flow is interrupted. Ruby is prepared to handle such problems with its own built-in exceptions, but you can handle them in your own way with exception handling. Ruby's exception handling model is similar to the C++ and Java models. Table 10 shows a comparison of the keywords or methods used to perform exception handling in all three languages.

Table 10. C++, Java and Ruby exception handling compared

C++	Java	Ruby
try {}	try {}	begin/end
catch {}	catch {}	rescue keyword (or catch method)
Not applicable	finally	ensure
throw	throw	raise (or throw method)

The rescue and ensure Clauses

Handle errors/exceptions by using the rescue and ensure clauses:

```
begin
    eval "1 / 0"
rescue ZeroDivisionError
    puts "Oops. You tried to divide by zero again."
    exit 1
ensure
    puts "Tsk. Tsk."
end
```

The eval method (from Kernel) evaluates a string as a Ruby statement. The result is disastrous, but this time the rescue clause catches the error, gives you a custom report in the form of the Oops string, and exits the program. (exit is another Kernel method; the argument 1 is a catchall for general errors.) You can have more than one ensure clause if your program calls for it.

Instead of giving its default message, that is, ZeroDivisionError: divided by 0, Ruby returns the message in rescue, plus the message in ensure. Even though the program exited at the end of the rescue clause, ensure yields its block, no matter what.

The raise Method

You don't have to wait for Ruby to raise an exception: you can raise one on your own with the raise method from Kernel. If things go haywire in a program, you can raise an exception with raise:

```
bad_dog = true

if bad_dog
  raise StandardError, "bad doggy"
else
  arf_arf
end
StandardError: bad doggy
```

If called without arguments, raise raises a RuntimeError if there was no previous exception. If raise has only a String argument, it raises a RuntimeError with the argument as a message. If the first argument is an exception, such as StandardError, the exception is raised with the given message, if such a message is present.

The catch and throw Methods

Kernel also has the catch and throw methods. catch executes a block that will properly terminate if there is no accompanying throw. If a throw accompanies catch, Ruby searches for a catch that has the same symbol as the throw. catch will then return the value given to throw, if present.

The following program is an adaptation of an example that came with the *ri* documentation for catch. throw sends a message to catch if n is less than or equal to 0:

```ruby
#!/usr/bin/env ruby

def limit( n )
  puts n
  throw :done if n <= 0
  limit( n-1 )
end

catch( :done ) { limit( 5 ) }
```

Object Class

These public methods are in the Object class, the base class for Ruby. This documentation is adapted and abbreviated from *http://www.ruby-doc.org/core/classes/Object.html*, where you can find code examples and longer explanations. Object includes the Kernel module, whose methods are listed in the next section.

Object Instance Methods

obj == *other* **[or]** *obj*.equal?(*other*) **[or]** *obj*.eql?(*other*)

At the Object level, == returns true only if *obj* and *other* are the same object. Typically, this method is overridden in descendant classes to provide class-specific meaning. Unlike ==, the equal? method should never be overridden by subclasses: it is used to determine object identity (that is, a.equal?(b) if and only if a is the same object as b). The eql? method returns true if *obj* and *other* have the same value.

obj === *other*

For class Object, effectively the same as calling ==, but typically overridden by descendants to provide meaningful semantics in case statements.

obj =~ *other*

Overridden by descendants (notably Regexp and String) to provide meaningful pattern-match semantics.

obj.__id__ **[or]** *obj*.object_id

Returns an integer identifier for *obj*. The same number will be returned on all calls to id for a given object, and no two active objects will share an id. Object#object_id is a different concept from the :name notation, which returns the symbol id of name. Replaces the deprecated Object#id.

obj.class

Returns the class of *obj*, now preferred over Object#type, because an object's type in Ruby is only loosely tied to that object's class. This method must always be called with an explicit receiver, because class is also a reserved word in Ruby.

obj.clone

Produces a shallow copy of *obj*—the instance variables of *obj* are copied, but not the objects they reference. Copies the frozen and tainted state of *obj*. See also the discussion under Object#dup.

obj.display(*port*=$>)

  Prints *obj* on the given port (default $>).

obj.dup

  Produces a shallow copy of *obj*—the instance variables of *obj* are copied, but not the objects they reference. dup copies the tainted state of *obj*.

obj.equal?(*other*) **[or]** *obj*.eql?(*other*) **[or]** *obj* == *other*

  See ==.

obj.eql?(*other*) **[or]** *obj* == *other* **[or]** *obj*.equal?(*other*)

  See ==.

obj.extend(*module*, ...)

  Adds to *obj* the instance methods from each *module* given as a parameter.

obj.freeze

  Prevents further modifications to *obj*. A TypeError will be raised if modification is attempted. There is no way to unfreeze a frozen object. See also Object#frozen?.

obj.frozen?

  Returns the freeze status of *obj*.

obj.hash

  Generates a Fixnum hash value for this object.

obj.id

  Soon-to-be deprecated version of Object#object_id.

obj.inspect

  Returns a string containing a human-readable representation of *obj*. If not overridden, uses the to_s method to generate the string.

obj.instance_eval(*string* [, *filename* [, *lineno*]]) **[or]**
obj.instance_eval { | | | *block* }

  Evaluates a string containing Ruby source code, or the given *block*, within the context of the receiver (*obj*). In order to set the context, the variable self is set to *obj* while the code is executing, giving the code access to *obj*'s instance variables. In the version of instance_eval that takes a string, the optional second and third parameters supply a *filename* and starting line number *lineno* that are used when reporting compilation errors.

obj.instance_of?(class)
> Returns true if *obj* is an instance of the given class. See also Object#kind_of?.

obj.instance_variable_defined?(symbol)
> Returns true if the given instance variable is defined in *obj*.

obj.instance_variable_get(symbol)
> Returns the value of the given instance variable, or nil if the instance variable is not set.

obj.instance_variable_set(*symbol, obj*)
> Sets the instance variable named by *symbol* to object, thereby frustrating the efforts of the class's author to attempt to provide proper encapsulation. The variable did not have to exist prior to this call.

obj.instance_variables
> Returns an array of instance variable names for the receiver.

obj.is_a?(*class*) **[or]** obj.kind_of?(*class*)
> Returns true if *class* is the class of *obj*, or if *class* is one of the superclasses of *obj* or modules included in *obj*.

obj.method(sym)
> Looks up the named method as a receiver in *obj*, returning a Method object (or raising NameError). The Method object acts as a closure in *obj*'s object instance, so instance variables and the value of self remain available.

obj.methods
> Returns a list of the names of methods publicly accessible in *obj*. This will include all the methods accessible in the ancestors of *obj*.

obj.nil? **[or]** nil.nil? **[or]** *anything_else*.nil?
 Returns true if receiver is nil. Only the object nil
 responds true to nil?.

obj.private_methods(*all*=true)
 Returns the list of private methods accessible to *obj*. If
 the *all* parameter is set to false, only those methods in
 the receiver will be listed.

obj.protected_methods(*all*=true)
 Returns the list of protected methods accessible to *obj*. If
 the *all* parameter is set to false, only those methods in
 the receiver will be listed.

obj.public_methods(all=true)
 Returns the list of public methods accessible to *obj*. If the
 all parameter is set to false, only those methods in the
 receiver will be listed.

obj.remove_instance_variable(symbol)
 Removes the named instance variable from *obj*, returning that variable's value.

obj.respond_to?(*symbol*, *include_private*=false)
 Returns true if *obj* responds to the given method. Private methods are included in the search only if the
 optional second parameter evaluates to true.

obj.send(*symbol* [, *args*...]) **[or]**
obj.__send__(*symbol* [, *args*...])
 Invokes the method identified by *symbol*, passing it any
 arguments specified. You can use __send__ if the name
 send clashes with an existing method in *obj*.

obj.singleton_method_added(*symbol*)
 Invoked as a callback whenever a singleton method is
 added to the receiver.

obj.singleton_method_removed(*symbol*)
 Invoked as a callback whenever a singleton method is
 removed from the receiver.

---

obj.singleton_method_undefined(*symbol*)

> Invoked as a callback whenever a singleton method is undefined in the receiver.

obj.singleton_methods(*all*=true)

> Returns an array of the names of singleton methods for *obj*. If the optional all parameter is true, the list will include methods in modules included in *obj*.

obj.taint

> Marks *obj* as tainted—if the $SAFE level is set appropriately, many method calls which might alter the running program's environment will refuse to accept tainted strings.

obj.tainted?

> Returns true if the object is tainted.

obj.to_a

> Returns an array representation of *obj*. For objects of class Object and others that don't explicitly override the method, the return value is an array containing self. However, this latter behavior will soon be obsolete.

obj.to_enum(*method* = :each, **args*) **[or]**
obj.enum_for(*method* = :each, **args*)

> Returns   Enumerable::Enumerator.new(self,   method, *args).

obj.to_s

> Returns a string representing *obj*. The default to_s prints the object's class and an encoding of the object id. As a special case, the top-level object that is the initial execution context of Ruby programs returns main.

obj.type

> Deprecated synonym for Object#class.

obj.untaint

> Removes the taint from *obj*.

Kernel Module

These public methods are in the Kernel module, the module that is included in the Object class, the base class of Ruby. This documentation is adapted and abbreviated from *http://www.ruby-doc.org/core/classes/Kernel.html*, where you can find code examples and longer explanations:

Array(*arg*)
  Returns *arg* as an Array.

Float(*arg*)
  Returns *arg* converted to a float.

Integer(*arg*)
  Converts *arg* to a Fixnum or Bignum.

String(*arg*)
  Converts *arg* to a String by calling its to_s method.

URI(*uri_str*)
  Alias for URI.parse.

\`*cmd*\`
  Returns the standard output of running *cmd* in a subshell.

abort **[or]** Kernel::abort **[or]** Process::abort
  Terminate execution immediately, effectively by calling Kernel.exit(1).

at_exit { *block* }
  Converts block to a Proc object (and therefore binds it at the point of call) and registers it for execution when the program exits.

autoload(*module, filename*)
  Registers *filename* to be loaded (using Kernel::require) the first time that module—which may be a String or a symbol—is accessed.

binding
  Returns a Binding object, describing the variable and method bindings at the point of call.

block_given? **[or]** iterator?
> Returns true if yield would execute a block in the current context. The iterator? form is mildly deprecated.

callcc { |*cont*| block }
> Generates a continuation object, which it passes to the associated block.

caller(*start*=1)
> Returns the current execution stack—an array containing strings in the form file:line or file:line: in method. The optional *start* parameter determines the number of initial stack entries to omit from the result.

catch(*symbol*) { | | *block* }
> If a throw is executed, Ruby searches up its stack for a catch block with a tag corresponding to the throw's symbol.

chomp **[or]** chomp(*string*)
> Equivalent to $_ = $_.chomp(string). See String#chomp.

chomp! **[or]** chomp!(*string*)
> Equivalent to $_.chomp!(string). See String#chomp!.

chop
> Equivalent to ($_.dup).chop!, except nil is never returned. See String#chop!.

chop!
> Equivalent to $_.chop!.

eval(*string* [, *binding* [, *filename* [, *lineno*]]])
> Evaluates the Ruby expression(s) in string. If *binding* is given, the evaluation is performed in its context. The binding may be a Binding object or a Proc object. If the optional filename and lineno parameters are present, they will be used when reporting syntax errors.

exec(*command* [, *arg*, …])
> Replaces the current process by running the given external command.

exit(*integer=0*) **[or]** Kernel::exit(*integer=0*) **[or]**
Process::exit(*integer=0*)
> Initiates the termination of the Ruby script by raising the
> SystemExit exception.

Process.exit!(*fixnum=-1*)
> Exits the process immediately. *fixnum* is returned to the
> underlying system as the exit status.

fail **[or]** fail(*string*) **[or]** fail(*exception* [, *string* [,
array]])
> See raise.

Kernel.fork {{ *block* }} **[or]** Process.fork {{ *block* }}
> Creates a subprocess. If a block is specified, that block is
> run in the subprocess, and the subprocess terminates
> with a status of zero. Otherwise, the fork call returns
> twice, once in the parent, returning the process ID of the
> child, and once in the child, returning nil.

format(*format_string* [, arguments...]) **[or]**
sprintf(*format_string* [, *arguments*...])
> See sprintf.

gets(*separator=$/*)
> Returns (and assigns to $_) the next line from the list of
> files in ARGV (or $*), or from standard input if no files are
> present on the command line. Returns nil at end of file.
> The optional argument specifies the record separator.

global_variables
> Returns an array of the names of global variables.

gsub(*pattern, replacement*) **[or]** gsub(*pattern*) { |...| *block* }
> Equivalent to $_.gsub except that $_ receives the modi-
> fied result.

gsub!(*pattern, replacement*) **[or]** gsub!(*pattern*) { |...| *block* }
> Equivalent to Kernel::gsub, except nil is returned if $_ is
> not modified.

iterator?
> See block_given?.

proc { |...| *block* } **[or]** lambda { |...| *block* }
    Equivalent to Proc.new, except the resulting Proc objects
    check the number of parameters passed when called.

load(*filename, wrap=false*)
    Loads and executes the Ruby program in the file
    filename.

local_variables
    Returns the names of the current local variables.

loop { |...| *block* }
    Repeatedly executes the block.

obj.method_missing(*symbol* [, **args*])
    Invoked by Ruby when *obj* is sent a message it cannot
    handle. *symbol* is the symbol for the method called, and
    args are any arguments that were passed to it.

open(*path* [, *mode* [, *perm*]]) **[or]**
open(*path* [, *mode* [, *perm*]]) |*io*| *block* }
    Creates an IO object connected to the given stream, file,
    or subprocess.

p(*obj*, ...)
    For each obj, directly writes obj.inspect followed by the
    current output record separator to the program's stan-
    dard output.

pretty_inspect( )
    Returns a pretty printed object as a string.

print(*obj*, ...)
    Prints each object in turn to $stdout.

printf(*io*, *string* [, *obj* ...]) **[or]** printf(*string* [, *obj* ...])
    Equivalent to io.write(sprintf(*string*, *obj*, ...) or
    $stdout.write(sprintf(*string*, *obj*, ...).

proc { |...| *block* }
    See lambda.

putc(*int*)
    Equivalent to $stdout.putc(*int*).

puts(*obj*, ...)
    Equivalent to $stdout.puts(*obj*, ...).

raise **[or]** raise(*string*) **[or]**
raise(*exception* [, *string* [, *array*]]) **[or]** fail **[or]**
fail(*string*) **[or]** fail(*exception* [, *string* [, *array*]])
    With no arguments, raises the exception in $! or raises a
    RuntimeError if $! is nil. With a single String argument,
    raises a RuntimeError with the string as a message. Other-
    wise, the first parameter should be the name of an
    Exception class (or an object that returns an Exception
    object when sent an exception message). The optional
    second parameter sets the message associated with the
    exception, and the third parameter is an array of call-
    back information. Exceptions are caught by the rescue
    clause of begin/end blocks.

rand(*max=0*)
    Converts *max* to an integer using max1 = max.to_i.abs. If
    the result is zero, returns a pseudorandom floating-point
    number greater than or equal to 0.0 and less than 1.0.
    Otherwise, returns a pseudorandom integer greater than
    or equal to zero and less than max1. Kernel::srand may be
    used to ensure repeatable sequences of random numbers
    between different runs of the program.

readline(*separator=$/*)
    Equivalent to Kernel::gets, except readline raises
    EOFError at end of file.

readlines(*separator=$/*)
    Returns an array containing the lines returned by calling
    Kernel.gets(*separator*) until the end of file.

require(*string*)
    Ruby tries to load the library named *string*, returning
    true if successful.

scan(*pattern*) **[or]** scan(*pattern*) { |////| *block* }
    Equivalent to calling $_.scan. See String#scan.

IO.select(*read_array* [, *write_array* [, *error_array*
[, *timeout*]]])
    See Kernel#select.

set_trace_func(*proc*) **[or]** set_trace_func(*nil*)
    Establishes *proc* as the handler for tracing, or disables
    tracing if the parameter is nil. *proc* takes up to six
    parameters: an event name, a filename, a line number, an
    object id, a binding, and the name of a class. *proc* is
    invoked whenever an event occurs.

sleep([*duration*])
    Suspends the current thread for *duration* seconds (which
    may be any number, including a Float with fractional
    seconds). Returns the actual number of seconds slept
    (rounded). Zero arguments causes sleep to sleep forever.

split([*pattern* [, *limit*]])
    Equivalent to $_.split(*pattern*, *limit*). See String#split.

sprintf(*format_string* [, *arguments*...]) **[or]**
format(*format_string* [, arguments...])
    Returns the string resulting from applying format_string
    to any additional arguments. Within the format string,
    any characters other than format sequences are copied to
    the result. A format sequence consists of a percent sign,
    followed by optional flags, width, and precision indica-
    tors, then terminated with a field type character. The
    field type controls how the corresponding sprintf argu-
    ment is to be interpreted, while the flags modify that
    interpretation. The field type characters and the flag
    characters are listed in the following tables. Examples:

```
# print a number in binary form
sprintf( "%b", 237 ) # => "11101101"

# refer to two arguments
sprintf("The integer %d is %08b in binary format.",
72, 72)

# refer to single argument with 1$
sprintf("The integer %1$d is %1$08b in binary format.",
72)
```

Sprintf flags and field types

Tables 11 and 12 list flags and field types for %, Kernel#sprintf (or its synonym Kernel#format).

Table 11. Flag characters for sprintf

Flag	For field types	Description
[space]	bdeEfgGiouxX	Places a space at the start of a positive number.
[1–9]$	All field types	Absolute number of an argument for this field.
#	beEfgGoxX	For the field b, result is prefixed with 0b; for o, with 0; for x, with 0x; for X, with 0X. For e, E, f, g, and G, adds decimal point. For g and G, does not remove trailing spaces.
+	bdeEfgGiouxX	Adds a leading plus sign (+) to positive numbers.
-	All field types	Left-justifies the result.
0	bdeEfgGiouxX	Pads result with zeros (0) instead of spaces.
*	All field types	Uses the next argument as the field width. If negative, left-justifies result. If asterisk (*) is followed by a number and a dollar sign ($), uses argument as width.

Table 12. Field types for sprintf

Field	Description
b	Converts a numeric argument to binary.
c	Converts a numeric argument (character code) to a character.
d	Converts a numeric argument to a decimal number. Same as i.
e	Converts a floating point argument into exponential notation, using one digit before the decimal point. Defaults to six fractional digits. Compare g.
E	Same as e, but uses E in result.
f	Converts a numeric argument to a floating-point number. Defaults to six fractional digits. Precision determines the number of fractional digits.
g	Converts a numeric argument to a floating point number using the exponential form if the exponent is less than -4 or greater than or equal to $precision$, otherwise in the form d.dddd. Compare e.
G	Same as g, but uses E in result.

Table 12. Field types for sprintf (continued)

Field	Description
i	Converts a numeric argument to a decimal number. Same as d.
o	Converts a numeric argument to octal.
p	Same as `argument.inspect` where `inspect` gives you a printable version of the argument, with special characters escaped.
s	Substitutes an argument as a string. If the format string contains *precision*, at most that many characters are copied in the substitution.
u	Treats argument as an unsigned decimal. Negative integers are displayed as a 32-bit two's complement plus one for the underlying architecture (for example, $2^{**}32+n$). Because Ruby has no inherent limit on the number of bits used to represent an integer, negative values are preceded by two leading periods, indicating an infinite number of leading sign bits.
x	Converts a numeric argument to hexadecimal with lowercase letters a through f. Negative numbers are displayed with two leading periods, indicating an infinite string of leading ffs.
X	Same as x, but uses uppercase letters A through F in the result. Negative numbers are displayed with two leading periods, indicating an infinite string of leading FFs.

srand(*number=0*)

> Seeds the pseudorandom number generator to the value of number.to_i.abs. If number is omitted or zero, seeds the generator using a combination of the time, the process id, and a sequence number. (This is also the behavior if Kernel::rand is called without previously calling srand, but without the sequence.) By setting the seed to a known value, scripts can be made deterministic during testing. The previous seed value is returned. Also see Kernel::rand.

sub(*pattern, replacement*) **[or]** sub(*pattern*) { block }

> Equivalent to $_.sub(args), except that $_ will be updated if substitution occurs.

sub!(*pattern, replacement*) **[or]** sub!(*pattern*) { |...| block }

> Equivalent to $_.sub!(*args*).

syscall(*fixnum* [, *args* ...])

> Calls the operating system function identified by *fixnum*, passing in the arguments, which must be either String objects, or Integer objects that ultimately fit within a native long.

system(*cmd* [, *arg*, ...])

> Executes *cmd* in a subshell, returning true if the command was found and ran successfully, false otherwise.

test(*int_cmd, file1* [, *file2*])

> Uses the integer aCmd to perform various tests on *file1* (Table 13) or on *file1* and *file2* (Table 14).

Table 13. File tests on single file

Test	Returns	Meaning
?A	Time	Last access time for file1.
?b	Boolean	True if file1 is a block device.
?c	Boolean	True if file1 is a character device.
?C	Time	Last change time for file1.
?d	Boolean	True if file1 exists and is a directory.
?e	Boolean	True if file1 exists.
?f	Boolean	True if file1 exists and is a regular file.
?g	Boolean	True if file1 has the \CF{setgid} bit set (false under Windows NT).
?G	Boolean	True if file1 exists and has a group ownership equal to the caller's group.
?k	Boolean	True if file1 exists and has the sticky bit set.
?l	Boolean	True if file1 exists and is a symbolic link.
?M	Time	Last modification time for file1.
?o	Boolean	True if file1 exists and is owned by the caller's effective uid.
?O	Boolean	True if file1 exists and is owned by the caller's real uid.
?p	Boolean	True if file1 exists and is a FIFO.
?r	Boolean	True if file1 is readable by the effective uid/gid of the caller.
?R	Boolean	True if file1 is readable by the real uid/gid of the caller.

Table 13. File tests on single file (continued)

Test	Returns	Meaning
?s	int/nil	If file1 has nonzero size, return the size, otherwise return nil.
?S	Boolean	True if file1 exists and is a socket.
?u	Boolean	True if file1 has the setuid bit set.
?w	Boolean	True if file1 exists and is writable by the effective uid/gid.
?W	Boolean	True if file1 exists and is writable by the real uid/gid.
?x	Boolean	True if file1 exists and is executable by the effective uid/gid.
?X	Boolean	True if file1 exists and is executable by the real uid/gid.
?z	Boolean	True if file1 exists and has a zero length.

Table 14. File tests for two files

Test	Returns	Description
?-	Boolean	True if file1 and file2 are identical.
?=	Boolean	True if the modification times of file1 and file2 are equal.
?<	Boolean	True if the modification time of file1 is prior to that of file2.
?>	Boolean	True if the modification time of file1 is after that of file2.

throw(*symbol* [, *obj*])

Transfers control to the end of the active catch block waiting for symbol. Raises NameError if there is no catch block for the symbol. The optional second parameter supplies a return value for the catch block, which otherwise defaults to nil. For examples, see Kernel::catch.

trace_var(*symbol*, *cmd*) **[or]** trace_var(*symbol*) { |*val*| *block* }

Controls tracing of assignments to global variables. The parameter symbol identifies the variable (as either a string name or a symbol identifier). cmd (which may be a string or a Proc object) or block is executed whenever the variable is assigned. The block or Proc object receives the variable's new value as a parameter. Also see Kernel:: untrace_var.

```
Signal.trap(signal, proc) [or]
Signal.trap(signal) { || block }
```
> Specifies the handling of signals. The first parameter is a
> signal name (a string such as SIGALRM, SIGUSR1, and so on)
> or a signal number. The characters SIG may be omitted
> from the signal name. The command or block specifies
> code to be run when the signal is raised. If the command
> is the string IGNORE or SIG_IGN, the signal will be ignored.
> If the command is DEFAULT or SIG_DFL, the operating sys-
> tem's default handler will be invoked. If the command is
> EXIT, the script will be terminated by the signal. Other-
> wise, the given command or block will be run. The spe-
> cial signal name EXIT or signal number zero will be
> invoked just prior to program termination. trap returns
> the previous handler for the given signal.

```
untrace_var(symbol [, cmd])
```
> Removes tracing for the specified command on the given
> global variable and returns nil. If no command is speci-
> fied, removes all tracing for that variable and returns an
> array containing the commands actually removed.

```
warn(msg)
```
> Displays the given message (followed by a newline) on
> STDERR unless warnings are disabled (for example, with
> the -W0 flag).

String Class

A String object in Ruby holds and manipulates an arbitrary
sequence of one or more bytes, typically representing characters that represent human language. Ruby has a built-in class
called String that defines a number of methods that are used
frequently when programming Ruby. Those methods are
listed at the end of this section. Following are string-related
features Ruby.

Expression Substitution

Expression substitution is a means of embedding the value of any Ruby expression into a string using #{ and }:

```
x, y, z = 12, 36, 72

puts "The value of x is #{ x }.

puts "The sum of x and y is #{ x + y }.

puts "The average was #{ (x + y + z)/3 }."
```

General Delimited Strings

With *general delimited strings*, you can create strings inside a pair of matching though arbitrary delimiter characters, e.g., !, (, {, <, etc., preceded by a percent character (%). Q, q, and x have special meanings. General delimited strings can be nested:

```
%{Ruby is fun.} # => "Ruby is fun."

%Q{ Ruby is fun. } # => " Ruby is fun. "

%q[Ruby is fun.] # equivalent to a single-quoted string

%x!ls! # => equivalent to back tick command output `ls`
```

Here Documents

Here documents allow you to quickly build multiline strings inside a nested pair of characters or words, preceded by <<. ", ', `, and - have special meanings. Here's an example:

```
# double-quoted string
puts <<x
To every thing there is a season,
and a time to every purpose
under the heaven.
x
```

```
# double-quoted string, assigned to variable
hamlet = <<"yorick"
Alas, poor Yorick! I knew him, Horatio: a fellow
of infinite jest, of most excellent fancy: he hath
borne me on his back a thousand times; and now, how
abhorred in my imagination it is! my gorge rims at
it. Here hung those lips that I have kissed I know
not how oft.
yorick

# single-quoted string
puts <<'Benedick'
Shall quips and sentences and these paper bullets of
the brain awe a man from the career of his humour?
No, the world must be peopled. When I said I would
die a bachelor, I did not think I should live till I
were married. Here comes Beatrice. By this day!
she's a fair lady: I do spy some marks of love in
her.
Benedick

# back-quoted string
dir = <<`ls`
ls -l
ls

# indented string
puts <<-cummings
  it's
  spring
  and
     the

        goat-footed

  balloonMan   whistles
  far
  and
  wee
cummings
```

Escape Characters

Table 15 is a list of escape or non-printable characters that can be represented with backslash notation. In a double-quoted string, an escape character is interpreted; in a single-quoted string, an escape character is preserved.

Table 15. Escape (non-printable) characters

Backslash notation	Hexadecimal character	Description
\a	0x07	Bell or alert
\b	0x08	Backspace
\c*x*		Control-*x*
\C-*x*		Control-*x*
\e	0x1b	Escape
\f	0x0c	Formfeed
\M-\C-*x*		Meta-Control-*x*
\n	0x0a	Newline
\nnn		Octal notation, where *n* is in the range 0–7
\r	0x0d	Carriage return
\s	0x20	Space
\t	0x09	Tab
\v	0x0b	Vertical tab
\x		Character *x*
\x*nn*		Hexadecimal notation, where *n* is in the range 0–9, a–f, or A–F

Character Encoding

It is often assumed that a character is represented by a single byte, which is not always the case. The default character set for Ruby is ASCII, whose characters may be represented by single bytes. If you use UTF-8, or another modern character set, characters may be represented in one to four bytes.

You can change your character set using $KCODE at the beginning of your program, like this:

```
$KCODE = 'u'
```

Table 16 shows possible values for $KCODE.

Table 16. $KCODE values

Code	Meaning
a	ASCII (same as none). This is the default.
e	EUC.
n	None (same as ASCII).
u	UTF-8.

Regular Expressions

A *regular expression* is a special sequence of characters that helps you match or find other strings or sets of strings, using a specialized syntax held in a pattern.

Given the opening lines of Shakespeare's 29th sonnet (a string that contains two lines, separated by a newline character, \n):

```
opening = "When in disgrace with fortune and men's eyes\nI
all alone beweep my outcast state,\n"
```

you can match the first line just by using a word in the pattern:

```
opening.grep(/men/) # => ["When in disgrace with fortune
and men's eyes\n"]
```

By the way, grep is not a String method; it comes from the Enumerable module, which the String class includes, so it is available for processing strings. grep takes a pattern as an argument, and can also take a block. See *http://www.ruby-doc.org/core/classes/Enumerable.html*.

When you use a pair of square brackets ([]), you can match any character in the brackets. Let's try to match the word *man* or *men* using []:

```
opening.grep(/m[ae]n/) # => ["When in disgrace with
fortune and men's eyes\n"]
```

It would also match a line with the word *man* in it.

Alternation lets you match alternate forms of a pattern using the bar (|):

```
opening.grep(/men|man/) # => ["When in disgrace with
fortune and men's eyes\n"]
```

Grouping uses parentheses to group a subexpression, like this one that contains an alternation:

```
opening.grep(/m(e|a)n/) # => ["When in disgrace with
fortune and men's eyes\n"]
```

Anchors anchor a pattern to the beginning (^) or end ($) of a line, like so:

```
opening.grep(/^When in/) # => ["When in disgrace with
fortune and men's eyes\n"]
opening.grep(/outcast state,$/) # => ["I all alone beweep
my outcast state,\n"]
```

The ^ means that a match is found when the text *When in* is at the beginning of a line, and $ will only match *outcast state* if it is found at the end of a line.

A way to specify the beginning and ending of strings in a pattern is with *shortcuts*. Shortcut syntax is brief, a single character preceded by a backslash. For example, the \d shortcut represents a digit; it is the same as using [0-9] but shorter. Similarly to ^, the shortcut \A matches the beginning of a string, not a line:

```
opening.grep(/\AWhen in/) # => ["When in disgrace with
fortune and men's eyes\n"]
```

The shortcut \z matches the end of a string, not a line, similarly to $:

```
opening.grep(/outcast state,\Z/) # => ["I all alone beweep
my outcast state,"]
```

The shortcut \Z matches the end of a string before the newline character, assuming that a newline character (\n) is at the end of the string (it won't work otherwise).

To match a phone number in the form (555)123-4567, sup-
pose that the string phone contains a phone number like this:

```
phone.grep(/[\(\d\d\d\)]?\d\d\d-\d\d\d\d/) # =>
["(555)123-4567"]
```

The backslash precedes the parentheses (\(...\)) to let the
regexp engine know that these are literal characters. Otherwise, the engine will see the parentheses as enclosing a subexpression. The three \ds in the parentheses represent three
digits. The hyphen (-) is just an unambiguous character, so
you can use it in the pattern as is.

The question mark (?) is a *repetition operator*. It means zero
or one occurrence of the previous pattern. So the phone number you are looking for can have an area code in parentheses
or not. The area code pattern is surrounded by [ ], so that the
? operator applies to the entire area code. Either form of the
phone number, with or without the area code, will work.
Here is a way to use ? with just a single character, *u*:

```
color.grep(/colou?r/) # => ["I think that colour is just
right for your office."]
```

The plus sign (+) operator indicates one or more of the previous patterns—in this case, digits:

```
phone.grep(/[\(\d+\)]?\d+-\d+/) # => ["(555)123-4567"]
```

An asterisk (*) operator indicates zero or more occurrences.

Braces ({}) let you specify the exact number of digits, like
\d{3} or \d{4}:

```
phone.grep(/[\(\d{3}\)]?\d{3}-\d{4}/)
# => ["(555)123-4567"]
```

It is also possible to indicate an *at least* amount with {m,},
and a minimum/maximum number with {*m,n*}.

The String class also has the =~ method and the !~ operator.
If =~ finds a match, it returns the offset position where the
match starts in the string:

```
color =~ /colou?r/ # => 13
```

The !~ operator returns true if it *does not* match the string, false otherwise.

```
color !~ /colou?r/ # => false
```

Also of interest are the Regexp and MatchData classes. The Regexp class (*http://www.ruby-doc.org/core/classes/Regexp.html*) lets you create a regular expression object. The MatchData class (*http://www.ruby-doc.org/core/classes/MatchData.html*) provides the special $- variable, which encapsulates all search results from a pattern match.

Table 17 lists the regular expression syntax that is available in Ruby.

Table 17. Regular expressions in Ruby

Pattern	Description
/pattern/options	Pattern *pattern* in slashes, followed by optional options, one or more of: i = case-insensitive; o = substitute once; x = ignore whitespace, allow comments; m = match multiple lines, newlines as normal characters.
%r!pattern!	General delimited string for a regular expression, where ! can be an arbitrary character.
^	Matches beginning of line.
$	Matches end of line.
.	Matches any character.
\1...\9	Matches *n*th grouped subexpression.
\10	Matches *n*th grouped subexpression, if already matched; otherwise refers to octal representation of a character code.
\n, \r, \t, etc.	Matches character in backslash notation.
\w	Matches word character, same as [0-9A-Za-z_].
\W	Matches nonword character, same as [^0-9A-Za-z_].
\s	Matches whitespace character, same as [\t\n\r\f].
\S	Matches non-whitespace character, same as [^\t\n\r\f].
\d	Matches digit, same as [0-9].

Table 17. Regular expressions in Ruby (continued)

Pattern	Description
\D	Matches non-digit, same as [^0-9].
\A	Matches beginning of string.
\Z	Matches end of a string, or before newline at the end.
\z	Matches end of a string.
\b	Matches word boundary outside [], or backspace (0x08) inside [].
\B	Matches nonword boundary.
\G	Matches point where last match finished.
[..]	Matches any single character in brackets, such as [ch].
[^..]	Matches any single character *not* in brackets.
*	Matches 0 or more of previous regular expression.
*?	Matches 0 or more of previous regular expression (non-greedy).
+	Matches 1 or more of previous regular expression.
+?	Matches 1 or more of previous regular expression (non-greedy).
{m}	Matches exactly *m* number of previous regular expression.
{m,}	Matches at least *m* number of previous regular expression.
{m,n}	Matches at least *m* but at most *n* number of previous regular expression.
{m,n}?	Matches at least *m* but at most *n* number of previous regular expression (non-greedy).
?	Matches 0 or 1 of previous regular expression.
|	Alternation, such as color|colour.
( )	Grouping regular expressions or subexpression, such as col(o|ou)r.
(?#..)	Comment.
(?:..)	Grouping without back references (without remembering matched text).

Table 17. Regular expressions in Ruby (continued)

Pattern	Description
(?=..)	Specify position with pattern.
(?!..)	Specify position with pattern negation.
(?>..)	Matches independent pattern without backtracking.
(?imx)	Toggles i, m, or x options on.
(?-imx)	Toggles i, m, or x options off.
(?imx:..)	Toggles i, m, or x options on within parentheses.
(?-imx:..)	Toggles i, m, or x options off within parentheses.
(?ix-ix:)	Turns on (or off) i and x options within this non-capturing group.
[:alnum:]	POSIX character class for alphanumeric.
[:alpha:]	POSIX character class for uppercase and lowercase letters.
[:blank:]	POSIX character class for blank and tab.
[:cntrl:]	POSIX character class for Control characters.
[:digit:]	POSIX character class for digits.
[:graph:]	POSIX character class for printable characters (but not space).
[:lower:]	POSIX character class for lowercase letter.
[:print:]	POSIX character class for printable characters (space included).
[:punct:]	POSIX character class for printable characters (but not space and alphanumeric).
[:space:]	POSIX character class for whitespace.
[:upper:]	POSIX character class for uppercase letter.
[:xdigit:]	POSIX character class for hex digit, A–F, a–f, 0–9.

String Methods

Following are the public String methods, adapted and abbreviated from *http://www.ruby-doc.org/core/classes/String.html*, and formatted and printed here for your convenience.

String class methods

new [String.new(*str*="")]
 Returns a new string object containing a copy of *str*.

String instance methods

str % *arg*
 Formats a string using a format specification. *arg* must be an array if it contains more than one substitution. For information on the format specification, see sprintf under "Kernel Module."

str * *integer*
 Returns a new string containing *integer* times *str*. In other words, *str* is repeated *integer* times.

str + *other_str*
 Concatenates *other_str* to *str*.

str << *fixnum* **[or]** *str* << *obj*
 Concatenates an object to *str*. If the object is a Fixnum in the range 0–255, it is converted to a character. Compare concat.

str <=> *other_str*
 Compares *str* with *other_str*, returning -1 (less than), 0 (equal), or 1 (greater than). The comparison is case-sensitive.

str == *obj*
 Tests *str* and *obj* for equality. If *obj* is not a String, returns false; returns true if *str* <=> *obj* returns 0.

str =~ *obj*
 Matches *str* against a regular expression pattern *obj*. Returns the position where the match starts; otherwise, false.

str[*fixnum*] **[or]** *str*[*fixnum,fixnum*] **[or]** *str*[*range*] **[or]**
str[*regexp*] **[or]** *str*[*regexp, fixnum*] **[or]** *str*[*other_str*]
 References *str*, using the following arguments: one Fixnum, returns a character code at *fixnum*; two Fixnums,

returns a substring starting at an offset (first *fixnum*) to length (second *fixnum*); *range*, returns a substring in the range; *regexp* returns portion of matched string; *regexp* with *fixnum*, returns matched data at *fixnum*; *other_str* returns substring matching *other_str*. A negative Fixnum starts at end of string with -1. Compare slice.

str[*fixnum*] = *fixnum* **[or]** *str*[*fixnum*] = *new_str* **[or]**
str[*fixnum, fixnum*] = *new_str* **[or]** *str*[*range*] = *aString* **[or]**
str[*regexp*] = *new_str* **[or]** *str*[*regexp, fixnum*] = *new_str* **[or]**
str[*other_str*] = *new_str*]

Replace (assign) all or part of a string. Synonym of slice!.

str.capitalize
  Capitalizes a string.

str.capitalize!
  Same as capitalize, but changes are made in place.

str.casecmp
  Makes a case-insensitive comparison of strings.

str.center
  Centers a string.

str.chomp
  Removes the record separator ($/), usually \n, from the end of a string. If no record separator exists, does nothing. Compare chop.

str.chomp!
  Same as chomp, but changes are made in place.

str.chop
  Removes the last character in *str*. Compare chomp.

str.chop!
  Same as chop, but changes are made in place. Compare chomp.

str.concat(*other_str*)
  Concatenates *other_str* to *str*. Compare <<, +.

str.count(str, ...)

> Counts one or more sets of characters. If there is more than one set of characters, counts the intersection of those sets.

str.crypt(*other_str*)

> Applies a one-way cryptographic hash to *str*. The argument is the salt string, which should be two characters long, each character in the range a–z, A–Z, 0–9, . or /.

str.delete(*other_str*, ...)

> Returns a copy of str with all characters in the intersection of its arguments deleted.

str.delete!(*other_str*, ...)

> Same as delete, but changes are made in place.

str.downcase

> Returns a copy of *str* with all uppercase letters replaced with lowercase.

str.downcase!

> Same as downcase, but changes are made in place. Compare upcase!.

str.dump

> Returns a version of *str* with all nonprinting characters replaced by \nnn notation and all special characters escaped.

str.each(*separator*=$/) { |*substr*| *block* }

> Splits *str* using argument as the record separator ($/ by default), passing each substring to the supplied block. Compare each_byte, each_line.

str.each_byte { |*fixnum*| *block* }

> Passes each byte from *str* to the block, returning each byte as a decimal representation of the byte.

str.each_line(*separator*=$/) { |*substr*| *block* }

> Splits *str* using argument as the record separator ($/ by default), passing each substring to the supplied block. Compare each.

---

str.empty?

> Returns true if *str* is empty (has a zero length).

str.eql?(other)

> Two strings are equal if the have the same length and content.

str.gsub(pattern, replacement) **[or]**
str.gsub(pattern) { |match| block }

> Returns a copy of *str* with all occurrences of pattern replaced with either replacement or the value of the block. The pattern will typically be a Regexp; if it is a String then no regular expression metacharacters will be interpreted (that is, /\d/ will match a digit, but '\d' will match a backslash followed by a 'd').

str.gsub!(pattern, replacement) **[or]** str.gsub!(pattern)
{ |match| block }

> Performs the substitutions of String#gsub in place, returning str, or nil if no substitutions were performed.

str.hash

> Returns a hash based on the string's length and content.

str.hex

> Treats leading characters from str as a string of hexadecimal digits (with an optional sign and an optional 0x) and returns the corresponding number. Zero is returned on error.

str.include? *other_str* **[or]** str.include? fixnum

> Returns true if *str* contains the given string or character.

str.index(substring [, offset]) **[or]**
str.index(fixnum [, offset]) **[or]**
str.index(regexp [, offset])

> Returns the index of the first occurrence of the given substring, character (*fixnum*), or pattern (regexp) in *str*. Returns nil if not found. If the second parameter is present, it specifies the position in the string to begin the search.

`str.insert(index, other_str)`

Inserts *other_str* before the character at the given index, modifying `str`. Negative indices count from the end of the string, and insert after the given character. The intent is to insert a string so that it starts at the given index.

`str.inspect`

Returns a printable version of `str`, with special characters escaped.

`str.intern` **[or]** `str.to_sym`

Returns the Symbol corresponding to `str`, creating the symbol if it did not previously exist.

`str.length`

Returns the length of `str`. Compare size.

`str.ljust(integer, padstr=' ')`

If *integer* is greater than the length of str, returns a new String of length *integer* with `str` left-justified and padded with *padstr*; otherwise, returns str.

`str.lstrip`

Returns a copy of `str` with leading whitespace removed. See also String#rstrip and String#strip.

`str.lstrip!`

Removes leading whitespace from `str`, returning nil if no change was made. See also String#rstrip! and String#strip!.

`str.match(pattern)`

Converts pattern to a Regexp (if it isn't already one), then invokes its match method on `str`.

`str.oct`

Treats leading characters of `str` as a string of octal digits (with an optional sign) and returns the corresponding number. Returns 0 if the conversion fails.

`str.replace(other_str)`

Replaces the contents and taintedness of `str` with the corresponding values in *other_str*.

str.reverse
> Returns a new string with the characters from *str* in reverse order.

str.reverse!
> Reverses *str* in place.

str.rindex(substring [, fixnum]) **[or]**
str.rindex(fixnum [, fixnum]) **[or]**
str.rindex(regexp [, fixnum])
> Returns the index of the last occurrence of the given substring, character (*fixnum*), or pattern (regexp) in *str*. Returns nil if not found. If the second parameter is present, it specifies the position in the string to end the search—characters beyond this point won't be considered.

str.rjust(*integer, padstr*=' ')
> If *integer* is greater than the length of *str*, returns a new String of length *integer* with *str* right-justified and padded with padstr; otherwise, returns *str*.

str.rstrip
> Returns a copy of *str* with trailing whitespace removed. See also String#lstrip and String#strip.

str.rstrip!
> Removes trailing whitespace from *str*, returning nil if no change was made. See also String#lstrip! and String#strip!.

str.scan(*pattern*) **[or]**
str.scan(*pattern*) { |*match*, ...| *block* }
> Both forms iterate through *str*, matching the pattern (which may be a Regexp or a String). For each match, a result is generated and either added to the result array or passed to the block. If the pattern contains no groups, each individual result consists of the matched string, $&. If the pattern contains groups, each individual result is itself an array containing one entry per group.

str.slice(*fixnum*) **[or]** *str*.slice(*fixnum, fixnum*) **[or]**
str.slice(*range*) **[or]** *str*.slice(*regexp*) **[or]**
str.slice(*regexp, fixnum*) **[or]** *str*.slice(*other_str*)
    See *str*[*fixnum*], etc.

str.slice!(fixnum) **[or]** *str*.slice!(fixnum, fixnum) **[or]**
str.slice!(range) **[or]** *str*.slice!(regexp) **[or]**
str.slice!(other_str)
    Deletes the specified portion from *str*, and returns the
    portion deleted. The forms that take a Fixnum will raise
    an IndexError if the value is out of range; the Range form
    will raise a RangeError, and the Regexp and String forms
    will silently ignore the assignment.

str.split(*pattern*=$;, [*limit*])
    Divides *str* into substrings based on a delimiter, return-
    ing an array of these substrings.

    If *pattern* is a String, then its contents are used as the
    delimiter when splitting *str*. If *pattern* is a single space,
    str is split on whitespace, with leading whitespace and
    runs of contiguous whitespace characters ignored.

    If *pattern* is a Regexp, *str* is divided where the pattern
    matches. Whenever the pattern matches a zero-length
    string, *str* is split into individual characters.

    If *pattern* is omitted, the value of $; is used. If $; is nil
    (which is the default), *str* is split on whitespace as if ` `
    were specified.

    If the *limit* parameter is omitted, trailing null fields are
    suppressed. If *limit* is a positive number, at most that
    number of fields will be returned (if *limit* is 1, the entire
    string is returned as the only entry in an array). If nega-
    tive, there is no limit to the number of fields returned,
    and trailing null fields are not suppressed.

str.squeeze([*other_str*]*)
    Builds a set of characters from the *other_str* parame-
    ter(s) using the procedure described for String#count.
    Returns a new string where runs of the same character

that occur in this set are replaced by a single character. If no arguments are given, all runs of identical characters are replaced by a single character.

`str.squeeze!([other_str]*)`

Squeezes str in place, returning either str, or nil if no changes were made.

`str.strip`

Returns a copy of *str* with leading and trailing whitespace removed.

`str.strip!`

Removes leading and trailing whitespace from *str*. Returns nil if *str* was not altered.

`str.sub(pattern, replacement)` **[or]**
`str.sub(pattern) { |match| block }`

Returns a copy of str with the first occurrence of *pattern* replaced with either *replacement* or the value of the block. The pattern will typically be a Regexp; if it is a String then no regular expression metacharacters will be interpreted.

`str.sub!(pattern, replacement)` **[or]**
`str.sub!(pattern) { |match| block }`

Performs the substitutions of String#sub in place, returning str, or nil if no substitutions were performed.

`str.succ` **[or]** `str.next`

Returns the successor to *str*.

`str.succ!` **[or]** `str.next!`

Equivalent to String#succ, but modifies the receiver in place.

`str.sum(n=16)`

Returns a basic *n*-bit checksum of the characters in str, where *n* is the optional Fixnum parameter, defaulting to 16. The result is simply the sum of the binary value of each character in str modulo 2n - 1. This is not a particularly good checksum.

str.swapcase

> Returns a copy of *str* with uppercase alphabetic charac-
> ters converted to lowercase and lowercase characters
> converted to uppercase.

str.swapcase!

> Equivalent to String#swapcase, but modifies the receiver
> in place, returning *str*, or nil if no changes were made.

str.to_f

> Returns the result of interpreting leading characters in
> *str* as a floating-point number. Extraneous characters
> past the end of a valid number are ignored. If there is not
> a valid number at the start of *str*, 0.0 is returned. This
> method never raises an exception.

str.to_i(*base*=10)

> Returns the result of interpreting leading characters in
> str as an integer base (base 2, 8, 10, or 16). Extraneous
> characters past the end of a valid number are ignored. If
> there is not a valid number at the start of *str*, 0 is
> returned. This method never raises an exception.

str.to_s **[or]** *str*.to_str

> Returns the receiver.

str.tr(*from_str*, *to_str*)

> Returns a copy of *str* with the characters in *from_str*
> replaced by the corresponding characters in *to_str*. If
> *to_str* is shorter than *from_str*, it is padded with its last
> character. Both strings may use the c1–c2 notation to
> denote ranges of characters, and *from_str* may start with
> a ^, which denotes all characters except those listed.

str.tr!(*from_str*, *to_str*)

> Translates *str* in place, using the same rules as
> String#tr. Returns *str*, or nil if no changes were made.

`str.tr_s(`*`from_str, to_str`*`)`

  Processes a copy of *str* as described under `String#tr`, then removes duplicate characters in regions that were affected by the translation.

`str.tr_s!(`*`from_str, to_str`*`)`

  Performs `String#tr_s` processing on *str* in place, returning *str*, or `nil` if no changes were made.

`str.unpack(`*`format`*`)`

  Decodes *str* (which may contain binary data) according to the format string, returning an array of each value extracted. The format string consists of a sequence of single-character directives, summarized in Table 18. Each directive may be followed by a number, indicating the number of times to repeat with this directive. An asterisk (*) will use up all remaining elements. The directives sSiIlL may each be followed by an underscore (_) to use the underlying platform's native size for the specified type; otherwise, it uses a platform-independent consistent size. Spaces are ignored in the format string. See also `Array#pack`.

`str.upcase`

  Returns a copy of *str* with all lowercase letters replaced with their uppercase counterparts. The operation is locale insensitive—only characters *a* to *z* are affected.

`str.upcase!`

  Changes the contents of `str` to uppercase, returning `nil` if no changes are made.

`str.upto(`*`other_str`*`) { |`*`s`*`| `*`block`* `}`

  Iterates through successive values, starting at *str* and ending at *other_str* inclusive, passing each value in turn to the block. The `String#succ` method is used to generate each value.

String unpack directives

Table 18 lists unpack directives for method String#unpack.

Table 18. String unpack directives

Directive	Returns	Description
A	String	With trailing nulls and spaces removed.
a	String	String.
B	String	Extract bits from each character (most significant bit first).
b	String	Extract bits from each character (least significant bit first).
C	Fixnum	Extract a character as an unsigned integer.
c	Fixnum	Extract a character as an integer.
D, d	Float	Treat sizeof(double) characters as a native double.
E	Float	Treat sizeof(double) characters as a double in little-endian byte order.
e	Float	Treat sizeof(float) characters as a float in little-endian byte order.
F, f	Float	Treat sizeof(float) characters as a native float.
G	Float	Treat sizeof(double) characters as a double in network byte order.
g	Float	Treat sizeof(float) characters as a float in network byte order.
H	String	Extract hex nibbles from each character (most significant bit first).
h	String	Extract hex nibbles from each character (least significant bit first).
I	Integer	Treat sizeof(int) (modified by _) successive characters as an unsigned native integer.
i	Integer	Treat sizeof(int) (modified by _) successive characters as a signed native integer.
L	Integer	Treat four (modified by _) successive characters as an unsigned native long integer.

Table 18. String unpack directives (continued)

Directive	Returns	Description
l	Integer	Treat four (modified by _) successive characters as a signed native long integer.
M	String	Quoted-printable.
m	String	Base64-encoded.
N	Integer	Treat four characters as an unsigned long in network byte order.
n	Fixnum	Treat two characters as an unsigned short in network byte order.
P	String	Treat sizeof(char *) characters as a pointer, and return \emph{len} characters from the referenced location.
p	String	Treat sizeof(char *) characters as a pointer to a null-terminated string.
Q	Integer	Treat eight characters as an unsigned quad word (64 bits).
q	Integer	Treat eight characters as a signed quad word (64 bits).
S	Fixnum	Treat two (different if _ used) successive characters as an unsigned short in native byte order.
s	Fixnum	Treat two (different if _ used) successive characters as a signed short in native byte order.
U	Integer	UTF-8 characters as unsigned integers.
u	String	UU-encoded.
V	Fixnum	Treat four characters as an unsigned long in little-endian byte order.
v	Fixnum	Treat two characters as an unsigned short in little-endian byte order.
w	Integer	BER-compressed integer (see Array.pack).
X		Skip backward one character.
x		Skip forward one character.
Z	String	With trailing nulls removed up to first null with *.
@		Skip to the offset given by the length argument.

Array Class

The `Array` class is one of Ruby's built-in classes. *Arrays* are compact, ordered collections of objects. Ruby arrays can hold objects such as `String`, `Integer`, `Fixnum`, `Hash`, `Symbol`, even other `Array` objects. Any object that Ruby can create, it can hold in an array. Each element in an array is associated with and referred to by an *index* (also known as a *subscript* in other languages). Array elements are automatically indexed (numbered) with an integer (`Fixnum`), starting with 0, then numbered consecutively, adding 1 for each additional element. In certain instances, you can refer to the last element of an array with -1, the second to last with -2, and so forth. That's handy. Ruby arrays are not as rigid as arrays in other languages. With static, compiled programming languages, you have to guess the ultimate size of the array at the time it is created. Not so with Ruby—arrays grow automatically.

Creating Arrays

There are many ways to create or initialize an array. One way is with the `new` class method:

```
months = Array.new
```

You can set the size of an array (the number of elements in an array) like this:

```
months = Array.new(12) [or] months = Array.new 12
```

The array `months` now has a size (or length) of 12 elements. You can return the size of an array with either the `size` or `length` methods:

```
months.size # => 12 [or] months.length # => 12
```

Another form of `new` lets you assign an object (such as a string) to each element in the array:

```
month = Array.new(12, "month")
```

You can also use a block with `new`, populating each element with what the block evaluates to:

```
num = Array.new(10) { |e| e = e * 2 }
```

giving you an array like this:

```
[0, 2, 4, 6, 8, 10, 12, 14, 16, 18]
```

There is another method of `Array`, `[]`. It works like this:

```
month_abbrv = Array.[]( "jan", "feb", "mar", "apr", "may",
"jun", "jul", "aug", "sep", "oct", "nov", "dec" )
```

or like this, dropping the dot (`.`) and parentheses (`( )`), which is possible because of Ruby's flexible method syntax:

```
month_abbrv = Array[ "jan", "feb", "mar", "apr", "may",
"jun", "jul", "aug", "sep", "oct", "nov", "dec" ]
```

An even simpler method for creating an array is this one, just using the square brackets:

```
months = [ nil, "January", "February", "March", "April",
"May", "June", "July", "August", "September", "October",
"November", "December" ]
```

The `Kernel` module, included in `Object`, has an `Array` method, which only accepts a single argument. Here the method takes a range as an argument to create an array of digits:

```
digits = Array(0..9) # => [1, 2, 3, 4, 5, 6, 7, 8, 9]
```

With the `%w` notation, you can define an array of strings. It assumes that all elements are strings (even nil), but it sure saves keystrokes (no typing quotes or commas):

```
months = %w[ nil January February March April May June
July August September October November December ]
```

To fill an array with numbers as strings using `%w`:

```
year = %w[ 2000 2001 2002 2003 2004 2005 2006 2007 2008
2009 ]
```

As numbers (not strings):

```
year = [2000, 2001, 2002, 2003, 2004, 2005, 2006, 2007,
2008, 2009]
```

You can even have an array that contains objects from different classes, not all just one type. For example, here's an array that contains four elements, each a different kind of object:

```
hodge_podge = ["January", 1, :year, [2006,01,01]]
```

Following are the public methods of the Array class, adapted and abbreviated from *http://www.ruby-doc.org/core/classes/Array.html*, where you will find examples and more detailed explanations of these methods.

Array Class Methods

Array.[](...) **[or]** Array[...] **[or]** [...]
>   Returns a new array populated with the given objects.

Array.new(*size*=0, *obj*=nil) **[or]** Array.new(*array*) **[or]**
Array.new(*size*) { |*index*| *block* }
>   Returns a new array. In the first form, the new array is empty. In the second it is created with *size* copies of *obj* (that is, *size* references to the same *obj*). The third form creates a copy of the array passed as a parameter. In the last form, an array of the given *size* is created. Each element in this array is calculated by passing the element's index to the given block and storing the return value.

Array Instance Methods

array & *other_array*
>   Returns a new array containing elements common to the two arrays, with no duplicates.

array * *int*   **[or]** *array* * *str*
>   Returns a new array built by concatenating the *int* copies of self. With a String argument, equivalent to self.join(str).

array + *other_array*
>   Returns a new array built by concatenating the two arrays together to produce a third array.

---

array - *other_array*

Returns a new array that is a copy of the original array, removing any items that also appear in *other_array*.

array | *other_array*

Returns a new array by joining *array* with *other_array*, removing duplicates.

array << *obj*

Pushes the given object onto the end of *array*. This expression returns the array itself, so several appends may be chained together.

array <=> *other_array*

Returns an integer (-1, 0, or +1) if this array is less than, equal to, or greater than *other_array*. Each object in each array is compared (using <=>). If any value isn't equal, then that inequality is the return value. If all the values found are equal, then the return value is based on a comparison of the array lengths. Thus, two arrays are equal according to Array#<=> if and only if they have the same length and the value of each element is equal to the value of the corresponding element in the other array.

array == *other_array*

Two arrays are equal if they contain the same number of elements and if each element is equal to (according to Object.==) the corresponding element in the other array.

array[*index*] **[or]** *array*[*start, length*] **[or]**
array[*range*] **[or]** *array*.slice(*index*) **[or]**
array.slice(*start, length*) **[or]** *array*.slice(*range*)

Returns the element at *index*, or returns a subarray starting at *start* and continuing for *length* elements, or returns a subarray specified by *range*. Negative indices count backward from the end of the array (-1 is the last element). Returns nil if the index (or starting index) is out of range.

`array[index] = obj` **[or]**
`array[start, length] = obj or an_array or nil` **[or]**
`array[range] = obj or an_array or nil`

> Sets the element at *index*, or replaces a subarray starting at *start* and continuing for *length* elements, or replaces a subarray specified by *range*. If indices are greater than the current capacity of the array, the array grows automatically. Negative indices will count backward from the end of the array. Inserts elements if *length* is zero. If *nil* is used in the second and third form, deletes elements from self. See also Array#push and Array#unshift.

`array.abbrev(pattern = nil)`

> Calculates the set of unambiguous abbreviations for the strings in self. If passed a pattern or a string, only the strings matching the pattern or starting with the string are considered.

`array.assoc(obj)`

> Searches through an array whose elements are also arrays comparing *obj* with the first element of each contained array using obj.==. Returns the first contained array that matches (that is, the first associated array), or nil if no match is found. See also Array#rassoc.

`array.at(index)`

> Returns the element at *index*. A negative index counts from the end of self. Returns nil if the index is out of range. See also Array#[]. (Array#at is slightly faster than Array#[], as it does not accept ranges and so on.)

`array.clear`

> Removes all elements from *array*.

`array.collect { |item| block }` **[or]**
`array.map { |item| block }`

> Invokes *block* once for each element of self. Creates a new array containing the values returned by the block.

array.collect! { |*item*| *block* } **[or]**
array.map! { |*item*| *block* }
> Invokes *block* once for each element of self, replacing the element with the value returned by *block*.

array.compact
> Returns a copy of self with all nil elements removed.

array.compact!
> Removes nil elements from array. Returns nil if no changes were made.

array.concat(*other_array*)
> Appends the elements in *other_array* to self.

array.delete(*obj*) **[or]** *array*.delete(*obj*) { *block* }
> Deletes items from self that are equal to *obj*. If the item is not found, returns nil. If the optional code block is given, returns the result of *block* if the item is not found.

array.delete_at(*index*)
> Deletes the element at the specified index, returning that element, or nil if the index is out of range. See also Array#slice!.

array.delete_if { |*item*| *block* }
> Deletes every element of self for which *block* evaluates to true.

array.each { |*item*| *block* }
> Calls *block* once for each element in self, passing that element as a parameter.

array.each_index { |index| block }
> Same as Array#each, but passes the *index* of the element instead of the element itself.

array.empty?
> Returns true if the self array contains no elements.

array.eql?(*other*)
> Returns true if *array* and *other* are the same object, or are both arrays with the same content.

array.fetch(*index*) **[or]** *array*.fetch(*index, default*) **[or]**
array.fetch(*index*) { |*index*| *block* }

> Tries to return the element at position *index*. If *index* lies
> outside the array, the first form throws an IndexError
> exception, the second form returns *default*, and the third
> form returns the value of invoking *block*, passing in *index*.
> Negative values of *index* count from the end of the array.

array.fill(*obj*) **[or]**
array.fill(*obj, start* [, *length*]) **[or]**
array.fill(*obj, range*) **[or]**
array.fill { |*index*| *block* } **[or]**
array.fill(*start* [, *length*]) { |*index*| *block* } **[or]**
array.fill(*range*) { |*index*| *block* }

> The first three forms set the selected elements of self
> (which may be the entire array) to *obj*. A start of nil is
> equivalent to zero. A length of nil is equivalent to
> self.length. The last three forms fill the array with the
> value of the block. The block is passed the absolute
> index of each element to be filled.

array.first **[or]** array.first(*n*)

> Returns the first element, or the first *n* elements, of the
> array. If the array is empty, the first form returns nil, and
> the second form returns an empty array.

array.flatten

> Returns a new array that is a one-dimensional flattening
> of this array (recursively). That is, for every element that
> is an array, extract its elements into the new array.

array.flatten!

> Flattens *array* in place. Returns nil if no modifications
> were made. (*array* contains no subarrays.)

array.frozen?

> Returns true if *array* is frozen (or temporarily frozen
> while being sorted).

array.hash

Compute a hash-code for *array*. Two arrays with the same content will have the same hash code (and will compare using eql?).

array.include?(*obj*)

Returns true if *obj* is present in self, false otherwise.

array.index(*obj*)

Returns the index of the first object in self that is == to *obj*. Returns nil if no match is found.

array.indexes(*i1, i2, ... iN*) **[or]**
array.indices(*i1, i2, ... iN*)

Deprecated; use Array#values_at.

array.indices(*i1, i2, ... iN*) **[or]**
array.indexes(*i1, i2, ... iN*)

Deprecated; use Array#values_at.

array.insert(*index, obj...*)

Inserts the given values before the element with the given *index* (which may be negative).

array.inspect

Creates a printable version of array.

array.join(*sep=$,*)

Returns a string created by converting each element of the array to a string, separated by *sep*.

array.last **[or]** *array*.last(*n*)

Returns the last element(s) of self. If *array* is empty, the first form returns nil.

array.length

Returns the number of elements in self. May be zero.

array.map { |*item*| *block* } **[or]**
array.collect { |item| block }

Invokes *block* once for each element of self. Creates a new array containing the values returned by the block.

---

array.map! { |*item*| *block* } **[or]**
array.collect! { |item| block }

> Invokes *block* once for each element of *array*, replacing the element with the value returned by block.

array.nitems

> Returns the number of non-nil elements in self. May be zero.

array.pack(*aTemplateString*)

> Packs the contents of *array* into a binary sequence according to the directives in *aTemplateString* (see Table 19). Directives A, a, and Z may be followed by a count, which gives the width of the resulting field. The remaining directives also may take a count, indicating the number of array elements to convert. If the count is an asterisk (*), all remaining array elements will be converted. Any of the directives sSiIlL may be followed by an underscore (_) to use the underlying platform's native size for the specified type; otherwise, they use a platform-independent size. Spaces are ignored in the template string. See also String#unpack.

Array pack directives

Table 19 lists pack directives for use with Array#pack.

Table 19. Array pack directives

Directive	Description
@	Moves to absolute position.
A	ASCII string (space padded, count is width).
a	ASCII string (null padded, count is width).
B	Bit string (descending bit order).
b	Bit string (ascending bit order).
C	Unsigned char.
c	Char.
D, d	Double-precision float, native format.

Table 19. Array pack directives (continued)

Directive	Description
E	Double-precision float, little-endian byte order.
e	Single-precision float, little-endian byte order.
F, f	Single-precision float, native format.
G	Double-precision float, network (big-endian) byte order.
g	Single-precision float, network (big-endian) byte order.
H	Hex string (high nibble first).
h	Hex string (low nibble first).
I	Unsigned integer.
i	Integer.
L	Unsigned long.
l	Long.
M	Quoted printable, MIME encoding (see RFC 2045).
m	Base64-encoded string.
N	Long, network (big-endian) byte order.
n	Short, network (big-endian) byte order.
P	Pointer to a structure (fixed-length string).
p	Pointer to a null-terminated string.
Q, q	64-bit number.
S	Unsigned short.
s	Short.
U	UTF-8.
u	UU-encoded string.
V	Long, little-endian byte order.
v	Short, little-endian byte order.
w	BER-compressed integer \fnm.
X	Back up a byte.
x	Null byte.
Z	Same as a, except that null is added with *.

array.pop

    Removes the last element from *array* and returns it, or nil if *array* is empty.

array.push(*obj,* ...)

    Pushes (appends) the given *obj* onto the end of this array. This expression returns the array itself, so several appends may be chained together.

array.rassoc(*key*)

    Searches through the array whose elements are also arrays. Compares *key* with the second element of each contained array using ==. Returns the first contained array that matches. See also Array#assoc.

array.reject { |*item*| *block* }

    Returns a new array containing the items *array* for which the block is not true.

array.reject! { |*item*| *block* }

    Deletes elements from *array* for which the block evaluates to true, but returns nil if no changes were made. Equivalent to Array#delete_if.

array.replace(*other_array*)

    Replaces the contents of *array* with the contents of *other_array*, truncating or expanding if necessary.

array.reverse

    Returns a new array containing *array*'s elements in reverse order.

array.reverse!

    Reverses *array* in place.

array.reverse_each {|item| *block* }

    Same as Array#each, but traverses *array* in reverse order.

array.rindex(*obj*)

    Returns the index of the last object in array == to *obj*. Returns nil if no match is found.

array.select {|*item*| *block* }
> Invokes the block passing in successive elements from array, returning an array containing those elements for which the block returns a true value.

array.shift
> Returns the first element of self and removes it (shifting all other elements down by one). Returns nil if the array is empty.

array.size
> Returns the length of *array* (number of elements). Alias for length.

array.slice(*index*) **[or]** *array*.slice(*start*, *length*) **[or]**
array.slice(*range*) **[or]** *array*[*index*] **[or]**
array[*start*, *length*] **[or]** *array*[*range*]
> Returns the element at *index*, or returns a subarray starting at *start* and continuing for *length* elements, or returns a subarray specified by *range*. Negative indices count backward from the end of the array (-1 is the last element). Returns nil if the *index* (or starting index) are out of range.

array.slice!(*index*) **[or]** *array*.slice!(*start*, *length*) **[or]**
array.slice!(*range*)
> Deletes the element(s) given by an *index* (optionally with a *length*) or by a *range*. Returns the deleted object, subarray, or nil if *index* is out of range.

array.sort **[or]** *array*.sort { | *a,b* | *block* }
> Returns a new array created by sorting self.

array.sort! **[or]** *array*.sort! { | *a,b* | *block* }
> Sorts self.

array.to_a
> Returns self. If called on a subclass of Array, converts the receiver to an Array object.

array.to_ary
> Returns self.

array.to_s
>   Returns self.join.

array.transpose
>   Assumes that self is an array of arrays and transposes the rows and columns.

array.uniq
>   Returns a new array by removing duplicate values in *array*.

array.uniq!
>   Removes duplicate elements from self. Returns nil if no changes are made (that is, no duplicates are found).

array.unshift(*obj*, ...)
>   Prepends objects to the front of array, other elements up one.

array.values_at(*selector*,...)
>   Returns an array containing the elements in self corresponding to the given *selector* (one or more). The *selectors* may be either integer indices or ranges. See also Array#select.

array.zip(*arg*, ...) **[or]** *array*.zip(*arg*, ...){ | *arr* | *block* }
>   Converts any arguments to arrays, then merges elements of *array* with corresponding elements from each argument.

Hash Class

A *hash* is an unordered collection of key-value pairs that look like this: "storm" => "tornado". A hash is similar to an Array, but instead of a default integer index starting at zero, the indexing is done with keys that can be made up from any Ruby object. In other words, you can use integer keys just like an Array, but you also have the option of using any Ruby object as a key, even an Array! (Hashes are actually implemented as arrays in Ruby.)

Hashes can be accessed by keys or by values, but usually by keys, which must be unique. If you attempt to access a hash with a key that does not exist, the method will return nil (unless the hash has a default value). The key-value pairs in a hash are not stored in the same order that they are inserted (the order you placed them in the hash), so don't be surprised if the contents of a hash look different than what you put in—the contents are not ordered like they are in an array.

Creating Hashes

As with arrays, there is a variety of ways to create hashes. You can create an empty hash with the new class method:

```
months = Hash.new
```

You can also use new to create a hash with a default value, which is otherwise just nil:

```
months = Hash.new( "month" ) [or] months = Hash.new "month"
```

When you access any key in a hash that has a default value, if the key or value doesn't exist, accessing the hash will return the default value:

```
months[0] [or] months[72] [or] months[234] # => "month"
```

Hash also has a class method [], which is called in one of two ways—with a comma separating the pairs, like this:

```
christmas_carol = Hash[ :name, "Ebenezer Scrooge", :
partner, "Jacob Marley", :employee, "Bob Cratchit", :
location, "London", :year, 1843 ] # => {:name=>"Ebenezer
Scrooge", :employee=>"Bob Cratchit", :year=>1843, :
partner=>"Jacob Marley", :location=>"London"}
```

or with =>:

```
christmas_carol = Hash[ :name => "Ebenezer Scrooge", :
partner => "Jacob Marley", :employee => "Bob Cratchit" =>:
location, "London", :year => 1843 ] # => {:name=>"Ebenezer
Scrooge", :employee=>"Bob Cratchit", :year=>1843, :
partner=>"Jacob Marley", :location=>"London"}
```

The easiest way to create a hash is just with curly braces:

```
months = { 1 => "January", 2 => "February", 3 => "March",
4 => "April", 5 => "May",  6 => "June", 7 => "July",
8 => "August", 9 => "September", 10 => "October",
11 => "November", 12 => "December" }
```

But that looks just like an array we created in the last chapter. What else could you do? Instead of integers, you could use strings for the keys:

```
month_a = { "jan" => "January", "feb" => "February",
"mar" => "March", "apr" => "April", "may" => "May",
"jun" => "June", "jul" => "July", "aug" => "August",
"sep" => "September", "oct" => "October", "nov" =>
"November", "dec" => "December" }
```

You can use any Ruby object as a key or value, even an array, so this will work: [1,"jan"] => "January".

Following are the public methods of the Hash class, adapted and abbreviated from *http://www.ruby-doc.org/core/classes/Hash.html*, where you will find examples and more detailed explanations of the methods.

Hash Class Methods

Hash[[key =>|, value]*]

Creates a new hash with zero or more key-values pairs, separated by => or ,.

Hash.new **[or]** Hash.new(*obj*) **[or]**
Hash.new { |*hash*, *key*| *block* }

Creates a new empty hash, a hash with a default value, or a hash via a block.

Hash Instance Methods

hash == *other_hash*

Tests whether two hashes are equal, based on whether they have the same number of key-value pairs, and whether the key-value pairs match the corresponding pair in each hash.

hash.[*key*]
> Using a key, references a value from *hash*. If the key is not found, returns a default value (see default, default=). Compare []=.

hash.[]=
> Compare store.

hash.clear
> Removes all key-value pairs from *hash*.

hash.default(*key* = nil)
> Returns the default value for *hash*, nil if not set by default=. ([] returns a default value if the key does not exist in *hash*.)

hash.default = *obj*
> Sets a default value for *hash*. Compare [], default.

hash.default_proc
> Returns a block if *hash* was created by a block.

hash.delete(*key*) **[or]** *array*.delete(*key*) { |*key*| *block* }
> Deletes a key-value pair from *hash* by *key*. If block is used, returns the result of a block if *pair* is not found. Compare delete_if.

hash.delete_if { |*key,value*| *block* }
> Deletes a key-value pair from *hash* for every pair the block evaluates to true. Compare delete, reject, reject!.

hash.each { |*key,value*| *block* }
> Iterates over *hash*, calling the block once for each key, passing the key-value as a two-element array.

hash.each_key { |*key*| *block* }
> Iterates over *hash*, calling the block once for each key, passing *key* as a parameter.

hash.each_key { |*key_value_array*| *block* }
> Iterates over *hash*, calling the block once for each key, passing the key and value as parameters.

hash.each_key { |*value*| *block* }

    Iterates over *hash*, calling the block once for each key, passing *value* as a parameter.

hash.empty?

    Tests whether *hash* is empty (contains no key-value pairs), returning true or false.

hash.fetch(*key* [, *default*]) **[or]**
hash.fetch(*key*) { | *key* | *block* }

    Returns a value from *hash* for the given *key*. If the key can't be found, and there are no other arguments, it raises an IndexError exception; if *default* is given, it is returned; if the optional block is specified, its result is returned.

hash.has_key?(*key*) **[or]** *hash*.include?(*key*) **[or]**
hash.key?(*key*) **[or]** *hash*.member?(*key*)

    Tests whether a given key is present in *hash*, returning true or false. Compare include?, key?, member?.

hash.has_value?

    Tests whether *hash* contains the given value. Compare value?

hash.index(*value*)

    Returns the key for the given value in *hash*, nil if no matching value is found.

hash.indexes

    Deprecated. See select.

hash.indices

    Deprecated. See select.

hash.inspect

    Returns a pretty print string version of *hash*.

hash.invert

    Creates a new hash, inverting keys and values from *hash*; that is, in the new hash, the keys from *hash* become values, and values become keys.

hash.keys

> Creates a new array with keys from *hash*.

hash.length

> Returns the size or length of *hash* as an integer. Compare size.

hash.merge(*other_hash*) **[or]**

hash.merge(*other_hash*) { |*key, oldval, newval*| *block* }

> Returns a new hash containing the contents of *hash* and *other_hash*, overwriting pairs in *hash* with duplicate keys with those from *other_hash*. Compare merge!, update.

hash.merge!(*other_hash*) **[or]**

hash.merge!(*other_hash*) { |*key, oldval, newval*| *block* }

> Same as merge, but changes are done in place.

hash.rehash

> Rebuilds *hash* based on the current values for each key. If values have changed since they were inserted, this method reindexes *hash*.

hash.reject { |*key, value*| *block* }

> Creates a new *hash* for every pair the block evaluates to true. Compare delete_if, select.

hash.reject! { |*key, value*| *block* }

> Same as *reject*, but changes are made in place.

hash.replace(*other_hash*)

> Replaces the contents of *hash* with the contents of *other_hash*.

hash.select { |*key, value*| *block* }

> Returns a new array consisting of key-value pairs from *hash* for which the block returns true. Compare values_at.

hash.shift

> Removes a key-value pair from *hash*, returning it as a two-element array.

hash.size

> Returns the size or length of *hash* as an integer. Compare length.

hash.sort

> Converts *hash* to a two-dimensional array containing arrays of key-value pairs, then sorts it as an array.

hash.store(*key, value*)

> Stores a key-value pair in *hash*. Compare []=.

hash.to_a

> Creates a two-dimensional array from *hash*. Each key-value pair is converted to an array, and all these arrays are stored in a containing array.

hash.to_hash

> Returns *hash* (self).

hash.to_s

> Converts *hash* to an array, then converts that array to a string.

hash.update(*other_hash*) **[or]**

hash.update(*other_hash*) {|*key, oldval, newval*| *block*}

> Returns a new hash containing the contents of *hash* and *other_hash*, overwriting pairs in *hash* with duplicate keys with those from *other_hash*. Compare merge, merge!.

hash.value?

> Tests whether *hash* contains the given value. Compare has_value?.

hash.values

> Returns a new array containing all the values of *hash*. Compare values_at.

hash.values_at(*obj*, ...)

> Returns a new array containing the values from *hash* that are associated with the given key or keys. Compare values.

Time Formatting Directives

These directives in Table 20 are used with the method Time#strftime.

Table 20. Directives for formatting time

Directive	Description
%a	The abbreviated weekday name (Sun).
%A	The full weekday name (Sunday).
%b	The abbreviated month name (Jan).
%B	The full month name (January).
%c	The preferred local date and time representation.
%d	Day of the month (01 to 31).
%H	Hour of the day, 24-hour clock (00 to 23).
%I	Hour of the day, 12-hour clock (01 to 12).
%j	Day of the year (001 to 366).
%m	Month of the year (01 to 12).
%M	Minute of the hour (00 to 59).
%p	Meridian indicator (AM or PM).
%S	Second of the minute (00 to 60).
%U	Week number of the current year, starting with the first Sunday as the first day of the first week (00 to 53).
%W	Week number of the current year, starting with the first Monday as the first day of the first week (00 to 53).
%w	Day of the week (Sunday is 0, 0 to 6).
%x	Preferred representation for the date alone, no time.
%X	Preferred representation for the time alone, no date.
%y	Year without a century (00 to 99).
%Y	Year with century.
%Z	Time zone name.
%%	Literal % character.

Interactive Ruby (irb)

Interactive Ruby or *irb* is an interactive programming environment that comes with Ruby. It was written by Keiju Ishitsuka. To invoke it, type *irb* at a shell or command prompt, and begin entering Ruby statements and expressions. Use exit or quit to exit *irb*. Here is a sample of *irb* evaluating a variety of expressions:

```
$ irb
irb(main):001:0> 23 + 27
=> 50
irb(main):002:0> 50 - 23
=> 27
irb(main):003:0> 10 * 5
=> 50
irb(main):004:0> 10**5
=> 100000
irb(main):005:0> 50 / 5
=> 10
irb(main):006:0> x = 1
=> 1
irb(main):007:0> x + 59
=> 60
irb(main):008:0> hi = "Hello, Matz!"
=> "Hello, Matz!"
irb(main):009:0> hi.each { |s| print s }
Hello, Matz!=> "Hello, Matz!"
irb(main):010:0> 1.upto( 10 ) { |n| print n, " " }
1 2 3 4 5 6 7 8 9 10 => 1
irb(main):011:0> 100 < 1_000
=> true
irb(main):012:0> class Hello
irb(main):013:1>   attr :hi, true
irb(main):014:1> end
=> nil
irb(main):015:0> h = Hello.new
=> #<Hello:0x3602cc>
irb(main):016:0> h.hi="Hello, Matz!"
=> "Hello, Matz!"
irb(main):017:0> h.hi
=> "Hello, Matz!"
```

```
irb(main):018:0> self
=> main
irb(main):019:0> self.class
=> Object
irb(main):020:0> exit
```

You can also invoke a single program with *irb*. After running
the program, *irb* exits:

```
$ cat hello.rb
#!/usr/bin/env ruby

class Hello
  def initialize( hello )
    @hello = hello
  end
  def hello
    @hello
  end
end

salute = Hello.new( "Hello, Matz!" )
puts salute.hello
$ irb hello.rb
hello.rb(main):001:0> #!/usr/bin/env ruby
hello.rb(main):002:0*
hello.rb(main):003:0* class Hello
hello.rb(main):004:1>   def initialize( hello )
hello.rb(main):005:2>     @hello = hello
hello.rb(main):006:2>   end
hello.rb(main):007:1>   def hello
hello.rb(main):008:2>     @hello
hello.rb(main):009:2>   end
hello.rb(main):010:1> end
=> nil
hello.rb(main):011:0>
hello.rb(main):012:0* salute = Hello.new( "Hello, Matz!" )
=> #<Hello:0x319f20 @hello="Hello, Matz!">
hello.rb(main):013:0> puts salute.hello
Hello, Matz!
=> nil
hello.rb(main):014:0> $
```

Usage:

```
irb[.rb] [options] [programfile] [arguments]
```

Options:

-f

Suppress reading of the file ~/.irbrc.

-m

bc mode (load mathn library so fractions or matrix are available).

-d

Set $DEBUG to true (same as ruby -d).

-r load-module

Same as ruby -r.

-I path

Specify $LOAD_PATH directory.

--inspect

Use inspect for output (default except for bc mode).

--noinspect

Don't use inspect for output.

--readline

Use Readline extension module.

--noreadline

Don't use Readline extension module.

--prompt prompt-mode (--prompt-mode prompt-mode)

Switch prompt mode. Predefined prompt modes are default, simple, xmp, and inf-ruby.

--inf-ruby-mode

Use prompt appropriate for inf-ruby-mode on Emacs. Suppresses --readline.

--simple-prompt

Simple prompt mode.

--noprompt

No prompt mode.

--tracer
    Display trace for each execution of commands.

--back-trace-limit *n*
    Display backtrace top *n* and tail *n*. The default value is 16.

--irb_debug *n*
    Set internal debug level to *n* (not for popular use).

-v *(--version)*.
    Print the version of irb.

Ruby Debugger

Usage:

    ruby -rdebug *filename[, ...]*

Commands:

b[reak] *[file:|class:](line|method)*
b[reak] *[class.](line|method)*
    Sets breakpoint to some position.

wat[ch] *expression*
    Sets watchpoint to some expression.

cat[ch] *(exception|off)*
    Sets catchpoint to an exception.

b[reak]
    Lists breakpoints.

cat[ch]
    Shows catchpoint.

del[ete][*nnn*]
    Deletes some or all breakpoints.

disp[lay] *expression*
    Adds expression into display expression list.

undisp[lay][*nnn*]
    Deletes one particular or all display expressions.

c[ont]
    Runs until program ends or hits breakpoint.

s[tep]*nnn*
    Steps (into methods) one line or until line *nnn*.

n[ext] *nnn*
    Goes over one line or until line *nnn*.

w[here]
    Displays frames.

f[rame]
    Alias for where.

l[ist][(-|*nn-mm*)
    Lists program, - lists backward.

nn-mm
    Lists given lines.

up[nn]
    Move to higher frame.

down[nn]
    Moves to lower frame.

fin[ish]
    Returns to outer frame.

tr[ace] (*on*|*off*)
    Sets trace mode of current thread.

tr[ace] (*on*|*off*) all
    Sets trace mode of all threads.

q[uit]
    Exits from debugger.

v[ar] g[lobal]
    Shows global variables.

v[ar] l[ocal]
    Shows local variables.

v[ar] i[nstance] *object*
    Shows instance variables of *object*.

v[ar] c[onst] *object*
    Shows constants of *object*.

m[ethod] i[nstance] *object*
    Shows methods of *object*.

m[ethod] (*class*|*module*)
    Shows instance methods of *class* or *module*.

th[read] l[ist]
    Lists all threads.

th[read] c[ur[rent]]
    Shows current thread.

th[read] [sw[itch]] *nnn*
    Switches thread context to *nnn*.

th[read] stop *nnn*
    Stops thread *nnn*.

th[read] resume *nnn*
    Resumes thread *nnn*.

p *expression*
    Evaluates *expression* and print its value.

h[elp]
    Prints this help.

everything else
    Evaluates.

Ruby Documentation

Ruby documentation refers to the documentation generated by RDoc (*http://rdoc.sourceforge.net*), a program that extracts documentation from Ruby source files, both from C and Ruby files.

The documentation is stored in comments in the source files and encoded so that RDoc can easily find it. RDoc can generate output as HTML, XML, *ri* (Ruby information), or Windows help (*chm*) files.

To see the RDoc-generated HTML documentation for Ruby, go to *http://www.ruby-doc.org/core*. If you have Ruby documentation installed on your system, which you likely do if you followed the installation instructions earlier in the book, you can type something like the following at a shell prompt to get formatted documentation in return. Type:

```
ri Kernel.print
```

and you will get this output:

```
----------------------------------------------------------
- Kernel#print
     print(obj, ...)    => nil
----------------------------------------------------------
--------------
     Prints each object in turn to +$stdout+. If the
output field
     separator (+$,+) is not +nil+, its contents will
appear between
     each field. If the output record separator (+$\+) is
not +nil+, it
     will be appended to the output. If no arguments are
given, prints
     +$_+. Objects that aren't strings will be converted
by calling
     their +to_s+ method.

         print "cat", [1,2,3], 99, "\n"
         $, = ", "
         $\ = "\n"
         print "cat", [1,2,3], 99

     _produces:_

         cat12399
         cat, 1, 2, 3, 99
```

Here are the RDOC formatting basics:

- Paragraphs in comments become paragraphs in the documentation.
- Words preceded by equals signs (such as `=== Example`) will be headings in the result, varying in font size depending on the number of equals signs—the more you use, the smaller the font of the heading. One `=` for a level-one heading, two `==` for a level two, and so forth.
- Indented text is formatted as code (typewriter font).
- Numbered lists (`1.`, `2.`, `3.`, etc.) become numbered lists.
- Labels followed by double colons (`::`) line up the text that follows in tabular form.
- The `:title:` directive lets RDoc know what you want the title of the XHTML document(s) to be (what goes inside `<head><title></title></head>`).
- Text enclosed by plus signs (`+new+`) will be shown in a typewriter (monospace) font in XHTML.
- Text enclosed in underscores (`_debt_`) will be shown in italics.
- Lines preceded by asterisks (`*`) will be set off as bullets in the XHTML.
- Marking up text in tt tags (`<tt>exec</tt>`) is the same as marking it up with plus signs (`+exec+`).
- Marking up text in i tags (`<i>wow!</i>`) is the same as marking it up with underscores (`_wow!_`).

RDoc Options

Usage:

```
rdoc [options] [names...]
```

names is a list of one or more filenames that you want to process with RDoc. Files are parsed, and the information they contain collected, before any output is produced. This allows cross-references between all files that are to be resolved.

If a filename on the command line is a directory, it is traversed. If no names are specified on the command line, all Ruby files in the current directory (and subdirectories) are processed.

Options:

`--accessor, -A` *accessorname*[,..]

Comma separated list of additional class methods that should be treated like attr_reader and friends. Option may be repeated. Each accessorname may have =text appended, in which case that text appears where the *r/w/ rw* appears for normal accessors.

`--all, -a`

Includes all methods (not just public) in the output.

`--charset, -c` *charset*

Specifies HTML character set.

`--debug, -D`

Displays internal information.

`--diagram, -d`

Generates diagrams showing modules and classes. You need *dot* V1.8.6 or later to use the --diagram option correctly. *Dot* is available from *http://www.research.att.com/ sw/tools/graphviz*.

`--exclude, -x` *pattern*

Does not process files or directories matching *pattern*. Files given explicitly on the command line will never be excluded.

`--extension, -E` *new=old*

Treats files ending with *.new* as if they ended with *.old*. Using '-E cgi=rb' will cause *xxx.cgi* to be parsed as a Ruby file.

`--fileboxes, -F`

Classes are put in boxes that represent files, where these classes reside. Classes shared between more than one file are shown with the list of files that share them. Silently discarded if --diagram option is not present as well. Experimental.

--fmt, -f *chm/html/ri/xml*
Sets the output formatter. Available output formatters are chm, html, ri, and xml.

--help, -h
Displays this usage information.

--help-output, -O
Explains the various output options.

--image-format, -I *gif/png/jpg/jpeg*
Sets output image format for diagrams. Can be png, gif, jpeg, jpg. If this option is omitted, png is used. Requires --diagram.

--include, -i *dir[,dir...]*
Sets (or adds to) the list of directories to be searched when satisfying :include: requests. Can be used more than once.

--inline-source, -S
Shows method source code inline, rather than via a pop-up link.

--line-numbers, -N
Includes line numbers in the source code.

--main, -m *name*
name will be the initial page displayed.

--merge, -M
When creating ri output, merges processed classes into previously documented classes of the name *name*.

--one-file, -1
Puts all the output into a single file.

--op, -o *dir*
Sets the output directory.

`--opname, -n` *name*
> Sets the name of the output. Has no effect for HTML.

`--promiscuous, -p`
> When documenting a file that contains a module or class also defined in other files, shows all stuff for that module/class in each file's page. By default, only shows stuff defined in that particular file.

`--quiet, -q`
> Doesn't show progress as we parse.

`--ri, -r`
> Generates output for use by ri. The files are stored in the *.rdoc* directory under your home directory unless overridden by a subsequent `--op` parameter, so no special privileges are needed.

`--ri-site, -R`
> Generates output for use by ri. The files are stored in a site-wide directory, making them accessible to others, so special privileges are needed.

`--ri-system, -Y`
> Generates output for use by ri. The files are stored in a system-level directory, making them accessible to others, so special privileges are needed. This option is intended to be used during Ruby installations.

`--show-hash, -H`
> A name of the form #name in a comment is a possible hyperlink to an instance method name. When displayed, the # is removed unless this option is specified.

`--style, -s` *stylesheet URL*
> Specifies the URL of a separate stylesheet.

`--tab-width, -w` *n*
> Sets the width of tab characters (default 8).

`--template, -T` *template name*
> Sets the template used when generating output.

--title, -t *text*
    Sets txt as the title for the output.

--version, -v
    Displays RDoc's version.

--webcvs, -W *url*
    Specifies a URL for linking to a web front-end to CVS. If the URL contains a '%s', the name of the current file will be substituted; if the URL doesn't contain a '%s', the filename will be appended to it.

For information on where the output goes, use:

```
rdoc --help-output
```

How RDoc generates output depends on the output formatter being used, and on the options you give:

- HTML output is normally produced into a number of separate files (one per class, module, and file, along with various indices). These files will appear in the directory given by the --op option (*doc/* by default).

- XML output by default is written to standard output. If an --opname option is given, the output will instead be written to a file with that name in the output directory.

- *.chm* files (Windows help files) are written in the --op directory. If an --opname parameter is present, that name is used; otherwise, the file will be called *rdoc.chm*.

RubyGems

RubyGems is a package utility for Ruby (*http://rubyforge.org/ projects/rubygems*). It was written by Jim Weirich. It installs Ruby software packages, and keeps them up to date. It is quite easy to learn and use, even easier than tools like the Unix/Linux tar utility (*http://www.gnu.org/software/tar*) or Java's jar utility (*http://java.sun.com/j2se/1.5.0/docs/tooldocs/ windows/jar.html*).

For more information, read the RubyGems documentation at *http://docs.rubygems.org*. The *RubyGems User Guide* (*http://docs.rubygems.org/read/book/1*) gives you most everything you need to know about using RubyGems. There is also a command reference (*http://docs.rubygems.org/read/book/2*).

If you don't have RubyGems installed, go to Chapter 3 of the *RubyGems User Guide* at *http://rubygems.org/read/chapter/3* for complete installation instructions.

Check to see whether RubyGems is installed:

```
$ gem --version
0.9.0
```

Get help on RubyGems:

```
$ gem --help

RubyGems is a sophisticated package manager for Ruby.
This is a basic help message containing pointers to more
information.

  Usage:
    gem -h/--help
    gem -v/--version
    gem command [arguments...] [options...]

  Examples:
    gem install rake
    gem list --local
    gem build package.gemspec
    gem help install

  Further help:
    gem help commands          list all 'gem' commands
    gem help examples          show some examples of
                               usage
    gem help <COMMAND>         show help on COMMAND
                               (e.g. 'gem help
                               install')

  Further information:
    http://rubygems.rubyforge.org
```

Get a list of RubyGems commands:

```
$ gem help commands
```

```
GEM commands are:
  build         Build a gem from a gemspec
  cert          Adjust RubyGems certificate settings
  check         Check installed gems
  cleanup       Cleanup old versions of installed gems in
                the local repository
  contents      Display the contents of the installed gems
  dependency    Show the dependencies of an installed gem
  environment   Display RubyGems environmental information
  help          Provide help on the 'gem' command
  install       Install a gem into the local repository
  list          Display all gems whose name starts with
                STRING
  query         Query gem information in local or remote
                repositories
  rdoc          Generates RDoc for pre-installed gems
  search        Display all gems whose name contains STRING
  specification Display gem specification (in yaml)
  uninstall     Uninstall a gem from the local repository
  unpack        Unpack an installed gem to the current
                directory
  update        Update the named gem (or all installed
                gems) in the local repository
```

For help on a particular command, use 'gem help COMMAND'.

Commands may be abbreviated, so long as they are
unambiguous.
e.g. 'gem i rake' is short for 'gem install rake'.

Get help on a specific RubyGems command:

```
$ gem help check
Usage: gem check [options]
```

```
  Options:
    -v, --verify FILE        Verify gem file against
                             its internal checksum
    -a, --alien              Report 'unmanaged' or
                             rogue files in the gem
                             repository
    -t, --test               Run unit tests for gem
    -V, --version            Specify version for
                             which to run unit tests
```

```
Common Options:
    --source URL              Use URL as the remote
                              source for gems
-p, --[no-]http-proxy [URL]   Use HTTP proxy for
                              remote operations
-h, --help                    Get help on this command
    --config-file FILE        Use this config file
                              instead of default
    --backtrace               Show stack backtrace on
                              errors
    --debug                   Turn on Ruby debugging

Summary:
  Check installed gems
```

Show RubyGems examples:

$ gem help examples

Some examples of 'gem' usage.

* Install 'rake', either from local directory or remote
  server:

      gem install rake

* Install 'rake', only from remote server:

      gem install rake --remote

* Install 'rake' from remote server, and run unit tests,
  and generate RDocs:

      gem install --remote rake --test --rdoc --ri

* Install 'rake', but only version 0.3.1, even if
  dependencies are not met, and into a specific directory:

      gem install rake --version 0.3.1 --force --install-dir
      $HOME/.gems

* List local gems whose name begins with 'D':

      gem list D

* List local and remote gems whose name contains 'log':

      gem search log --both

* List only remote gems whose name contains 'log':

      gem search log --remote

* Uninstall 'rake':

      gem uninstall rake

* Create a gem:

      See http://rubygems.rubyforge.org/wiki/wiki.
          pl?CreateAGemInTenMinutes

* See information about RubyGems:

      gem environment

List available remote RubyGems packages with the following (drop the --remote flag to see what you have locally):

```
$ gem list --remote

*** REMOTE GEMS ***
Need to update 17 gems from http://gems.rubyforge.org
.................
complete

abstract (1.0.0)
    a library which enables you to define abstract method
    in Ruby

ackbar (0.1.1, 0.1.0)
    ActiveRecord KirbyBase Adapter

action_profiler (1.0.0)
    A profiler for Rails controllers

actionmailer (1.3.3, 1.3.2, 1.3.1, 1.3.0, 1.2.5, 1.2.4,
1.2.3, 1.2.2, 1.2.1, 1.2.0, 1.1.5, 1.1.4, 1.1.3, 1.1.2,
1.1.1, 1.0.1, 1.0.0, 0.9.1, 0.9.0, 0.8.1, 0.8.0, 0.7.1,
0.7.0, 0.6.1, 0.6.0, 0.5.0, 0.4.0, 0.3.0)
    Service layer for easy email delivery and testing.
```

```
actionpack (1.13.3, 1.13.2, 1.13.1, 1.13.0, 1.12.5,
1.12.4, 1.12.3, 1.12.2, 1.12.1, 1.12.0, 1.11.2, 1.11.1,
1.11.0, 1.10.2, 1.10.1, 1.9.1, 1.9.0, 1.8.1, 1.8.0, 1.7.0,
1.6.0, 1.5.1, 1.5.0, 1.4.0, 1.3.1, 1.3.0, 1.2.0, 1.1.0,
1.0.1, 1.0.0, 0.9.5, 0.9.0, 0.8.5, 0.8.0, 0.7.9, 0.7.8,
0.7.7, 0.7.6, 0.7.5)
    Web-flow and rendering framework putting the VC in MVC.

actionservice (0.3.0, 0.2.102, 0.2.100, 0.2.99)
    Web service support for Action Pack.

actionwebservice (1.2.3, 1.2.2, 1.2.1, 1.2.0, 1.1.6,
1.1.5, 1.1.4, 1.1.3, 1.1.2, 1.1.1, 1.1.0, 1.0.0, 0.9.4,
0.9.3, 0.9.2, 0.9.1, 0.8.1, 0.8.0, 0.7.1, 0.7.0, 0.6.2,
0.6.1, 0.6.0, 0.5.0)
    Web service support for Action Pack.
```

[truncated]

Install or update Rake (make à la Ruby, discussed in the next section). You may need root privileges to do this (essentially, you'll need a root password). I use sudo (*http://www.gratisoft.us/sudo*) to do this:

$ sudo gem install rake

```
WARNING: Improper use of the sudo command could lead to
data loss or the deletion of important system files.
Please double-check your typing when using sudo. Type "man
sudo" for more information.

To proceed, enter your password, or type Ctrl-C to abort.

Password:
Bulk updating Gem source index for: http://gems.rubyforge.
org
Successfully installed rake-0.7.2
Installing ri documentation for rake-0.7.2...
Installing RDoc documentation for rake-0.7.2...
```

Rake

A build tool helps you build, compile, or otherwise process files, sometimes large numbers of them. Rake is a build tool like *make* (*http://www.gnu.org/software/make*) and Apache *ant* (*http://ant.apache.org*), but it is written in Ruby. It is used by Ruby many applications, not just Rails. Rails operations use Rake frequently, so it is worth mentioning here.

Rake uses a Rakefile to figure out what to do. A Rakefile contains named tasks. When you create a Rails project, a Rakefile is automatically created to help you deal with a variety of jobs, such as running tests and looking at project statistics. (After creating a Rails project with one of the tutorials below, while in the main Rails project directory, run rake --tasks or rails stats to get a flavor of what Rake does.)

Rake was written by Jim Weirich (*http://onestepback.org*). You'll find documentation on Rake at *http://rake.rubyforge.org*. Additionally, you'll find a good introduction to Rake, by Martin Fowler, at *http://www.martinfowler.com/articles/rake.html*.

Check to see whether Rake is present:

```
$ rake --version
rake, version 0.7.2
```

If this command fails, use RubyGems to install Rake, as shown in the previous section.

To run Rake help, type:

```
$ rake --help
```

Usage:

```
rake [-f rakefile] {options} targets...
```

Options:

`--classic-namespace` *(-C)*
    Put Task and FileTask in the top-level namespace.

`--dry-run` *(-n)*
    Do a dry run without executing actions.

`--help` *(-H)*
    Display this help message.

`--libdir=`*LIBDIR* *(-I)*
    Include *LIBDIR* in the search path for required modules.

`--nosearch` *(-N)*
    Do not search parent directories for the Rakefile.

`--prereqs` *(-P)*
    Display the tasks and dependencies, then exit.

`--quiet` *(-q)*
    Do not log messages to standard output.

`--rakefile` *(-f)*
    Use *FILE* as the Rakefile.

`--rakelibdir=`*RAKELIBDIR* *(-R)*
    Auto-import any *.rake* files in *RAKELIBDIR* (default is rakelib).

`--require=`*MODULE* *(-r)*
    Require *MODULE* before executing Rakefile.

`--silent` *(-s)*
    Like --quiet, but also suppresses the *in directory* announcement.

`--tasks` *(-T)*
    Display the tasks (matching optional PATTERN) with descriptions, then exit.

`--trace` *(-t)*
    Turn on invoke/execute tracing; enable full backtrace.

`--usage` *(-h)*
    Display usage.

`--verbose` *(-v)*
    Log message to standard output (default).

`--version` *(-V)*
    Display the program version.

Ruby Resources

http://www.ruby-lang.org
    Ruby language main site

http://www.rubyist.net/~matz
    Matz's blog (in Japanese)

http://www.ruby-doc.org
    Ruby documentation site

http://www.rubyonrails.org
    Ruby on Rails

http://railsconf.com
    Rails Conf

http://rubyforge.org
http://raa.ruby-lang.org
    Ruby source code repositories

http://www.rubycentral.com
    Ruby Central, sponsor of Ruby Conf

http://www.oreilly.com/catalog/0974514055/index.html
http://www.amazon.com/Programming-Ruby-Pragmatic-Programmers-Second/dp/0974514055
    Programming Ruby, Second Edition, by Dave Thomas et al.
    (Pragmatic)

*http://www.awprofessional.com/bookstore/product.
asp?isbn=0672328844&rl=1*
*http://www.amazon.com/Ruby-Way-Second-Addison-Wesley-
Professional/dp/0672328844*

> *The Ruby Way*, Second Edition, by Hal Fulton (Addison-Wesley)

http://poignantguide.net/ruby

> *Why's (Poignant) Guide to Ruby* by why the lucky stiff

*http://www.amazon.com/Cookbook-Cookbooks-OReilly-
Lucas-Carlson/dp/0596523696*
http://www.oreilly.com/catalog/rubyckbk

> *Ruby Cookbook* by Lucas Carlson and Leonard Richardson (O'Reilly)

Glossary

accessor

> A method for accessing data in a class that is usually inaccessible otherwise. Also called getter and setter methods.

Ajax

> Originally an abbreviation for Asynchronous JavaScript and XML. A web design technique that uses XMLHttpRequest to load data (often small bits of data) onto a web page without requiring the entire page to be refreshed from the server.

aliasing

> Using the Ruby keyword alias, you can alias a method, operator, or global constant by specifying an old and a new name.

ARGF

> An I/O-like stream that allows access to a virtual concatenation of all files provided on the command line, or standard input if no files are provided.

ARGV

An array that contains all of the command-line arguments passed to a program.

argument

Variables passed to a method. In the method call `hello ( name )`, the variable `name` is an argument. See method.

array

A data structure containing an ordered list of elements—any Ruby object—starting with an index of 0. Compare with hash.

ASCII

Abbreviation for American Standard Code for Information Interchange. ASCII is a character set representing 128 letters, numbers, symbols, and special codes, in the range 0–127. Each character can be represented by an 8-bit byte (octet). Ruby default. Set with `$KCODE = 'a'`. Compare with UTF-8.

block

A nameless function, always associated with a method call, contained in a pair of braces (`{}`) or do/end.

block comment

See comment.

C extensions

Ruby is written in the C programming language. You can extend Ruby with C code, perhaps for performance gains or to do some heavy lifting. For quick instructions on how to do this, see Peter Cooper's article "How to create a Ruby Extension in C in under 5 minutes" at *http://www.rubyinside.com/how-to-create-a-ruby-extension-in-c-in-under-5-minutes-100.html*.

carriage return

See newline.

child class

A class that is derived from a parent or superclass. Compare with superclass.

class

A collection of code, including methods and variables called members. The code in a class sets the rules for objects of the given class. See instance, module, object.

class variable

A variable that can be shared between objects of a given class. In Ruby, prefixed with two at signs, as in `@@count`. See global variable, instance variable, local variable.

closure

A nameless function or method. It is like a method within another method that refers to or shares variables with the enclosing or outer method. In Ruby, the closure or block is wrapped by braces (`{}`) or `do`/`end`, and depends on the associated method to work.

comment

Program text that is ignored by the Ruby interpreter. If it is preceded by a `#`, and not buried in double quotes, the text or line is ignored by the Ruby interpreter. Block comments, enclosed by `=begin`/`=code`, can contain comments that cover more than one line. These are also called embedded documents.

composability

The degree to which you can express logic by combining and recombining parts of a language (see "The Design of RELAX NG," by James Clark, at *http://www. thaiopensource.com/relaxng/design.html#section:5*).

concatenation

Joining or chaining together two strings performed in Ruby with the `+`, `<<`, and `concat` methods.

conditional expression

See ternary operator.

conditional statement
> Tests whether a given statement is true or false, executing code (or not) based on the outcome. Conditional statements are formed with keywords such as if, while, and unless.

constant
> In Ruby, a constant name is capitalized or all uppercase. It is not fixed as in other languages, though when you change the value of a constant, the Ruby interpreter warns you that the constant is already initialized. Compare with variable.

data structure
> Data stored in a computer in a way that (usually) allows efficient retrieval of the data. Arrays and hashes are examples of data structures.

database
> A systematic collection of information, stored on a computer. Ruby on Rails is a database-enabled web application framework.

default
> A value that is assigned automatically when interacting with code or a program.

each
> In Ruby, a method named each (or similarly, like each_line) iterates over a given block, processing the data piece by piece—by bytes, characters, lines, elements, and so forth, depending on the structure of the data. See block.

embedded document
> See comment.

embedded Ruby
> See ERB.

enumerable

> In Ruby, collection classes that have traversal and searching methods and sort capability. Methods include all?, any, find, grep, include?, max, member?, min, and sort.

error

> A problem or defect in code that usually causes a program to halt. Common errors in Ruby programs are identified with classes such as ArgumentError, EOFError, and ZeroDivisionError. Compare with exception.

ERB

> An abbreviation for Embedded Ruby. A technique, similar to JavaServer Pages, for embedding Ruby code in tags—such as <%= and %>—in text files, including HTML and XHTML, that is executed when the files are processed. Ruby on Rails makes extensive use of embedded Ruby. ERB is actually a built-in implementation of embedded Ruby, but other, faster implementations also exist, such as Erubis (*http://rubyforge.org/projects/erubis*).

eRuby

> See ERB.

exception

> Allows you to catch and manage runtime and other errors while programming. Managed with rescue, ensure, and raise. Compare with error.

expression

> A programming statement that includes keywords, operators, variables, and so forth, and returns a value.

expression substitution

> In Ruby, a syntax that allows you to embed expressions in strings and other contexts. The substitution is enclosed in #{ and }, and the result of the expression replaces the substitution in place when the code runs through the interpreter.

---

extension, file
>The part of the filename (if present) that follows the period. The conventional file extension for Ruby is *.rb*.

extension, C
>See C extensions.

file mode
>Depending on how it is set, determines the ability to read, write, and execute a file. One way you can set a file's mode is with `File.new` at the time the file is created.

float
>In Ruby, objects that represent real numbers, such as `1.0`. A floating-point number in Ruby is an instance of the `Float` class.

gem
>See RubyGems.

general delimited strings
>A technique for creating strings using `%!` and `!`, where `!` can be an arbitrary non-alphanumeric character. Alternative syntax: `%Q!string!` for double-quoted strings, `%q!string!` for single-quoted strings, and `%x!string!` for back-quoted strings.

getter method
>See accessor.

global variable
>A variable whose scope includes the entire program. Can be done with a singleton. Compare with class variable, instance variable, local variable, singleton.

graphical user interface
>See GUI.

GUI
>An abbreviation for graphical user interface. A user interface that focuses on graphics rather than text. Mac OS X is an example. Tcl/Tk is Ruby's built-in GUI library.

hash

> An unordered collection of data where keys and values are mapped. Compare with array.

hash code

> An integer calculated from an object. Identical objects have the same hash code. Generated by a hash method.

here document

> A technique that allows you to build strings from multiple lines, using <<*name/name* where *name* is an arbitrary name. Alternative syntax: <<"*string*"/*string* for double-quoted strings, <<'*string*'/*string* for single-quoted strings, <<`*string*`/*string* for back-quoted strings, and <<-*string/string* for indented strings.

hexadecimal

> A base-16 number, represented by the digits 0–9 and the letters A–F or a–f. Often prefixed with 0x. For example, the base-10 number 26 is represented as 0x1A in hexadecimal.

index

> An integer that numbers or identifies the elements in an array. Array indexes always start with 0. See array.

inheritance

> The ability of a class to inherit features from another class via the < operator. See multiple inheritance, single inheritance.

instance

> An object that is created when a class is instantiated, often with the new class method; for example, str = String.new creates an instance of the String class.

instance variable

> A variable associated with an instance of a class. In Ruby, instance variables are prefixed with a single at sign—for example, @name. See class variable, local variable, global variable.

I/O

An abbreviation for input/output. Refers to the flow of data to and from the computer, such as reading data to and from a file. The IO class is the basis for all of Ruby's I/O, and the File class is a subclass of IO.

key

A key is associated with a value in a hash. You can use keys to access hash values. See hash.

keyword

See reserved word.

lambda

In Ruby, a method that creates a Proc object that is bound to the current context and does parameter checking (checks the number) when called. See proc.

library

See standard library.

line-end character

See newline.

linefeed

See newline.

local variable

A variable with local scope, such as inside a method. You cannot access a local variable from outside of its scope. In Ruby, local variables begin with a lowercase letter or an underscore (_). num and _outer are examples of local variables. See class variable, global variable, instance variable.

loop

A repeatable iteration of one or more statements. Ruby uses for loops, and even has a loop method for such a task. A loop may be stopped (with break). Control then passes to the next statement in the program or a special location, or it may even exit the program. Kernel has a loop method.

main

> The initial, top-level execution context for Ruby programs. Test it by entering self in *irb*:

```
irb(main):001:0> self
=> main
```

match

> When a method finds its specified regular expression, it is said to match. See regular expression.

member

> Variables and methods are considered members of a class or object. See class, method, object, variable.

metaprogramming

> Programming that creates and/or manipulates other programs. Ruby's define_method method is an important tool that can be used in metaprogramming. Reflection is another capability that plays a role in metaprogramming. See reflection.

method

> A named collection of statements, with or without arguments, and a return value. A member of a class. See class.

mixin

> When a module is included in a class, it is mixed into the class, hence the name *mixin*. Using mixins helps overcome the problems that stem from multiple inheritance. See module.

mode, file

> See file mode.

module

> A module is like a class, but it cannot be instantiated like a class. A class can include a module so that when the class is instantiated, it gets the included module's methods and so forth. The methods from an included module become instance methods in the class that includes the module. This is called mixing in, and a module is referred to as a mixin. See class, mixin.

modulo

A division operation that returns the remainder of the operation. The percent sign (%) is used as the modulo operator.

multiple inheritance

When a class can inherit more than one class. C++, for example, supports multiple inheritance, which has disadvantages (such as name collision) that, in many opinions, outweigh the advantages. See single inheritance.

name collision

Names (identifiers) collide when they cannot be resolved unambiguously. A risk of multiple inheritance.

namespace

In Ruby, a module acts as a namespace. A namespace is a set of names—such as method names—that have a scope or context. A Ruby module associates a single name with a set of method and constant names. The module name can be used in classes in other modules. Generally, the scope or context of such a namespace is the class or module where the namespace (module name) is included. A Ruby class can also be considered a namespace.

newline

A character that ends a line, such as a linefeed (Mac OS X and Unix/Linux) or a combination of characters such as character return and linefeed (Windows).

nil

Empty, uninitialized, or invalid. `nil` is always `false`, but is not the same as zero. It is a pseudovariable, and an object of `NilClass`. See pseudovariable.

object

An instance of a class, a thing, an entity, or a concept that is represented in contiguous memory in a computer. See instance, class.

object-oriented programming

Refers to a programming practice that is based on organizing data with methods that can manipulate that data. The methods and data (members) are organized into classes that can be instantiated as objects. See class.

octal

A base-8 number, represented by the digits 0–7. Often prefixed with 0 (zero). For example, the decimal number 26 is represented as 32 in octal.

OOP

See object-oriented programming.

operators

Perform operations such as addition and subtraction. Ruby operators include, like other languages, + for addition, - for subtraction, * for multiplication, / for division, % for modulo, and so forth. Many Ruby operators are methods.

overloading

Method or function overloading is a practice in object-oriented programming that allows methods with the same name to operate on different kinds of data (methods or functions with the same name but different signatures). You can't really overload methods in Ruby without branching the logic inside the method. See overriding.

overriding

Redefining a method. The latest definition is the one recognized by the Ruby interpreter. Compare with overloading.

package

See RubyGems.

parent class

See superclass.

path

> The location of a file on a filesystem. Used to help locate files for opening, executing, and so forth. Contained in the PATH environment variable.

pattern

> A sequence of ordinary and special characters that enables a regular expression engine to locate a string. See regular expression.

pop

> A term related to a stack—a last-in, first-out (LIFO) data structure. When you pop an element off a stack, you are removing the last element first. You can pop elements off (out of) an array in Ruby. Compare with push.

push

> A term related to a stack—a last-in, first-out (LIFO) data structure. When you push an element onto a stack, you are adding an element onto the end of the array. You can push elements onto an array in Ruby. Compare with pop.

precision

> Refers to the preciseness with which a numerical quantity is expressed. The Precision module in Ruby enables you to convert numbers (float to integer, integer to float).

private

> A method that is marked private can only be accessed, or is only visible, within its own class. Compare with protected, public.

proc

> In Ruby, a procedure that is stored as an object, complete with context; an object of the Proc class. See lambda.

protected

A method that is marked protected can only be accessed or visible within its own class, or child classes. Compare with private, public.

pseudovariable

An object that looks like a variable and acts like a constant but can't be assigned a value. nil and self are examples of pseudovariables.

public

A method that is marked public (which is the default) is accessible or visible in its own class and from other classes. Compare with private, protected.

RAA

See Ruby Application Archive.

RDoc

A tool for generating documentation embedded in comments in Ruby source code. For more information, see *http://rdoc.sourceforge.net*.

Rails

See Ruby on Rails.

Rake

A build tool written in Ruby with capabilities like make, a predecessor. See *http://rake.rubyforge.org*.

random number

With the Kernel#rand or Kernel#srand methods, Ruby can generate an arbitrary, pseudorandom number.

range

In Ruby, a way of representing inclusive (..) and exclusive (...) ranges of objects, usually numbers. For example, 1..10 is a range of numbers from 1 to 10, inclusive; using ... instead of .. excludes the last value from the range.

rational number

A fraction. In Ruby, rational numbers are handled via the Rational class.

RoR

Abbreviation for Ruby on Rails. See Ruby on Rails.

receiver

An object that receives or is the context for the action that a method performs. In the method call `str.length`, `str` is the receiver of the length method.

reflection

The ability of a language such as Ruby to examine and manipulate itself. For example, the reflection method class from Object returns an object's class ("hello". class # => String).

regular expression

A concise sequence or pattern of special characters used to search for strings. See match.

reserved word

Another name for keyword. Reserved words such as begin, end, if, else, and so forth are set aside and have special meaning to the Ruby interpreter.

Ruby Application Archive

A web-based archive for Ruby applications. Not the same as RubyForge.

RubyForge

A web-based archive for Ruby applications. Not the same as Ruby Application Archive.

RubyGems

The premier packing system for Ruby applications. A RubyGems package is called a gem. It comes with Ruby (though you must choose to install it explicitly with certain installation procedures).

Ruby on Rails

A productive, popular web application framework written in Ruby. Matz, the inventor of Ruby, has called it Ruby's killer app.

self

A pseudovariable representing the current object or receiver invoked by a method. See pseudovariable, receiver.

setter method

See accessor.

single inheritance

When a class can inherit only one class, as opposed to multiple inheritance, which allows a class to inherit from multiple classes. See multiple inheritance.

singleton

A singleton class is tied to a particular object, can be instantiated only once, and is not distinguished by a prefixed name. A singleton method is tied to the singleton class. May be used like or in place of a class variable.

standard library

A library or collection of Ruby code containing packages that perform specialized tasks. Some example packages are REXML for XML processing, and Iconv for character set conversion. Online documentation is available at *http://ruby-doc.org/stdlib*.

statement

An instruction for a program to carry out.

string

A sequence of objects, usually symbols of human-readable characters.

substitution

See expression substitution.

superclass

> The parent class. A child class is derived from the parent or superclass. Compare with child class.

Tcl/Tk

> The Tcl scripting language with the Tk user interface toolkit, Ruby's built-in GUI library or system.

ternary operator

> An operator that takes three arguments separated by ? and :, a concise form of if/then/else. For example, `label = length == 1 ? " argument" : " arguments"`.

thread

> Ruby supports threading. Threading allows programs to execute multiple tasks simultaneously (or almost simultaneously) by slicing the time on the clock that runs the computer processor. The threads in Ruby are operating-system independent, so threading is available on all platforms that run Ruby, even if the OS doesn't support them.

Unicode

> An international character coding system that allows approximately 65,000 characters. See *http://www.unicode.org*.

UTF-8

> A character set, based on one to four bytes, that can describe most characters in human writing systems. Set with `$KCODE = 'n'`. Compare with ASCII.

variable

> An identifier or name that may be assigned to an object which in turn may hold a quantity or a value. See class variable, global variable, instance variable, local variable.

XML

> An abbreviation for *Extensible Markup Language*. A language specified by the W3C that enables you to create vocabularies using tags and other markup. Ruby uses REXML, Builder, and libxml to process XML.

Index

We'd like to hear your suggestions for improving our indexes. Send email to
index@oreilly.com.